Cakes & Desserts

Everyday Cookbook

STAR
FIRE

This is a Star Fire book
First published in 2006

06 08 10 09 07

1 3 5 7 9 10 8 6 4 2

Star Fire is part of
The Foundry Creative Media Company Limited
Crabtree Hall, Crabtree Lane, Fulham, London, SW6 6TY

Visit our website: www.star-fire.co.uk

ISBN-10: 1-84451-304-1 ISBN-13: 978-1-84451-304-8
Special Edition: ISBN-10: 1-84451-612-1 ISBN-13: 978-1-84451-612-4

The CIP record for this book is available from the British Library.

Printed in China

ACKNOWLEDGEMENTS

Publisher and Creative Director: Nick Wells
Editorial Planning: Rosanna Singler
Design and Production: Chris Herbert, Mike Spender, Colin Rudderham and Claire Walker

Authors: Catherine Atkinson, Juliet Barker, Gina Steer, Vicki Smallwood,
Carol Tennant, Mari Mererid Williams, Elizabeth Wolf-Cohen and Simone Wright
Editorial: Sara Goulding and Sara Robson
Photography: Colin Bowling, Paul Forrester and Stephen Brayne
Home Economists and Stylists: Jacqueline Bellefontaine,
Mandy Phipps, Vicki Smallwood and Penny Stephens

All props supplied by Barbara Stewart at Surfaces

NOTE
Recipes using uncooked eggs should be avoided by infants,
the elderly, pregnant women and anyone suffering from an illness.

Contents

Everyday Cakes

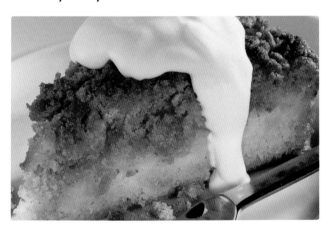

Cream Cakes & Gateaux

Desserts

Hygiene in the Kitchen

It is important to remember that many foods can carry some form of bacteria. In most cases, the worst it will lead to is a bout of food poisoning or gastroenteritis, although for certain people this can be serious. The risk can be reduced or eliminated, however, by good hygiene and proper cooking.

Do not buy food that is past its sell-by date and do not consume food that is past its use-by date. When buying food, use the eyes and nose. If the food looks tired, limp or a bad colour or it has a rank, acrid or simply bad smell, do not buy or eat it under any circumstances.

Take special care when preparing raw meat and fish. A separate chopping board should be used for each, and the knife, board and your hands should be thoroughly washed before handling or preparing any other food.

Regularly clean, defrost and clear out the refrigerator or freezer – it is worth checking the packaging to see exactly how long each product is safe to freeze. Avoid handling food if suffering from an upset stomach as bacteria can be passed on through food preparation.

Dish cloths and tea towels must be washed and changed regularly. Ideally use disposable cloths which should be replaced on a daily basis. More durable cloths should be left to soak in bleach, then washed in the washing machine at a high temperature.

Keep your hands, cooking utensils

and food preparation surfaces clean and do not allow pets to climb on to any work surfaces.

Buying

Avoid bulk buying where possible, especially fresh produce such as meat, poultry, fish, fruit and vegetables. Fresh foods lose their nutritional value rapidly, so buying a little at a time minimises loss of nutrients. It also means your fridge won't be so full, which reduces the effectiveness of the refrigeration process.

When buying prepackaged goods such as cans or pots of cream and yogurts, check that the packaging is intact and not damaged or pierced at all. Cans should not be dented, pierced or rusty. Check the sell-by dates even for cans and packets of dry ingredients such as flour and rice. Store fresh foods in the refrigerator as soon as possible – not in the car or the office.

When buying frozen foods, ensure that they are not heavily iced on the outside and that the contents feel completely frozen. Ensure that the frozen foods have been stored in the cabinet at the correct storage level and the temperature is below -18°C/-0.4°F. Pack in cool bags to transport home and place in the freezer as soon as possible after purchase.

Preparation

Make sure that all work surfaces and utensils are clean and dry. Hygiene should be given priority at all times. Separate chopping boards should be used for raw and cooked meats, fish and vegetables. Currently, a variety of good quality plastic boards come in various designs and colours. This makes differentiating easier and the plastic has the added hygienic advantage of being washable at high temperatures in the dishwasher.

If using the board for fish, first wash in cold water, then in hot to prevent odour. Also remember that knives and utensils should always be thoroughly cleaned after use.

When cooking, be particularly careful to keep cooked and raw food separate to avoid any contamination. It is worth washing all fruits and vegetables regardless of whether they are going to be eaten raw or lightly cooked.

This rule should apply even to prewashed herbs and salads.

Do not reheat food more than once. If using a microwave, always check that the food is piping hot all the way through – in theory, the food should reach 70°C/158°F and needs to be cooked at that temperature for at least three minutes to ensure that all bacteria are killed.

All poultry must be thoroughly thawed before using, including chicken and poussin. Remove the food to be thawed from the freezer and place in a shallow dish to contain the juices. Leave the food in the refrigerator until it is completely thawed. A 1.4 kg/3 lb whole chicken will take about 26–30 hours to thaw. To speed up the process, immerse the chicken in cold water, making sure that the water is changed regularly. When the joints can move freely and no ice crystals remain in the cavity, the bird is completely thawed.

Once thawed, remove the wrapper and pat the chicken dry. Place the chicken in a shallow dish, cover lightly and store as close to the base of the refrigerator as possible. The chicken should be cooked as soon as possible.

Some foods can be cooked from frozen including many prepacked foods such as soups, sauces, casseroles and breads. Where applicable follow the manufacturers' instructions.

Vegetables and fruits can also be cooked from frozen, but meats and fish should be thawed first. The only time food can be refrozen is when the food has been thoroughly thawed then cooked. Once the food has cooled then it can be frozen again, but it should only be stored for one month.

All poultry and game (except for duck) must be cooked thoroughly. When cooked, the juices will run clear on the thickest part of the bird – the best area to try is usually the thigh. Other meats, like minced meat and pork should be cooked right the way through. Fish should turn opaque, be firm in texture and break easily into large flakes.

When cooking leftovers, make sure they are reheated until piping hot and that any sauce or soup reaches boiling point first.

Storing, Refrigerating and Freezing

Meat, poultry, fish, seafood and dairy products should all be refrigerated. The temperature of the refrigerator should be between 1–5°C/34–41°F while the freezer temperature should not rise above -18°C/-0.4°F.

To ensure the optimum refrigerator and freezer temperature, avoid leaving the door open for long periods of time.

Try not to overstock the refrigerator as this reduces the airflow inside and therefore the effectiveness in cooling the food within.

When refrigerating cooked food, allow it to cool down quickly and completely before refrigerating. Hot food will raise the temperature of the refrigerator and possibly affect or spoil other food stored in it.

Food within the refrigerator and freezer should always be covered. Raw and cooked food should be stored in separate parts of the refrigerator. Cooked food should be kept on the top shelves of the refrigerator, while raw meat, poultry and fish should be placed on bottom shelves to avoid drips and cross-contamination. It is recommended that eggs should be refrigerated in order to maintain their freshness and shelf life.

Take care that frozen foods are not stored in the freezer for too long. Blanched vegetables can be stored for one month; beef, lamb, poultry and pork for six months and unblanched vegetables and fruits in syrup for a year. Oily fish and sausages should be stored for three months. Dairy products can last four to six months, while cakes and pastries should be kept in the freezer for three to six months.

High Risk Foods

Certain foods may carry risks to people who are considered vulnerable such as the elderly, the ill, pregnant women, babies, young infants and those suffering from a recurring illness.

It is advisable to avoid those foods listed below which belong to a higher-risk category.

There is a slight chance that some eggs carry the bacteria salmonella. Cook the eggs until both the yolk and the white are firm to eliminate this risk. Pay particular attention to dishes and products incorporating lightly cooked or raw eggs which should be eliminated from the diet. Hollandaise sauce, mayonnaise, mousses, soufflés and meringues all use raw or lightly

cooked eggs, as do custard-based dishes, ice creams and sorbets. These are all considered high-risk foods to the vulnerable groups mentioned above.

Certain meats and poultry also carry the potential risk of salmonella and so should be cooked thoroughly until the juices run clear and there is no pinkness left. Unpasteurised products such as milk, cheese (especially soft cheese), pâté, meat (both raw and cooked) all have the potential risk of listeria and should be avoided.

When buying seafood, buy from a reputable source which has a high turnover to ensure freshness. Fish should have bright clear eyes, shiny skin and bright pink or red gills. The fish should feel stiff to the touch, with a slight smell of sea air and iodine. The flesh of fish steaks and fillets should be translucent with no signs of discolouration. Molluscs such as scallops, clams and mussels are sold fresh and are still alive. Avoid any that are open or do not close when tapped lightly. In the same way, univalves such as cockles or winkles should withdraw back into their shells when lightly prodded. When choosing cephalopods such as squid and octopus they should have a firm flesh and pleasant sea smell.

As with all fish, whether it is shellfish or seafish, care is required when freezing it. It is imperative to check whether the fish has been frozen before. If it has been frozen, then it should not be frozen again under any circumstances.

Essential Ingredients

The quantities may differ, but basic baking ingredients do not vary greatly. Let us take a closer look at the baking ingredients that are essential.

Fat

Butter and firm block margarine are the fats most commonly used in baking. Others can also be used such as white vegetable fat, lard and oil. Low-fat spreads are not recommended for baking as they break down when cooked at a high temperature. Often it is a matter of personal preference which fat you choose when baking but there are a few guidelines that are important to remember.

Unsalted butter is the fat most commonly used in cake making, especially in rich fruit cakes and the heavier sponge cakes such as Madeira or chocolate torte. Unsalted butter gives a distinctive flavour to the cake. Some people favour margarine which imparts little or no flavour to the cake. As a rule, firm margarine and butter should not be used straight from the refrigerator but allowed to come to room temperature before using. Also, it should be beaten by itself first before creaming or rubbing in. Soft margarine is best suited to one-stage recipes. If oil is used care should be taken – it is a good idea to follow a specific recipe as the proportions of oil to flour and eggs are different.

Fat is an integral ingredient when making pastry, and again there are a few specific guidelines to bear in mind.

For shortcrust pastry the best results are achieved by using equal amounts of lard or white vegetable fat with butter or block margarine. The amount of fat used is always half the amount of flour. Other pastries use differing amounts of ingredients. Pâté sucrée (a sweet flan pastry) uses all butter with eggs and a little sugar, while flaky or puff pastry uses a larger proportion of fat to flour and relies on the folding and rolling during making to ensure that the pastry rises and flakes well. When using a recipe, refer to the instructions to obtain the best results.

Flour

A wide range of flour is available, all designed for specific jobs. Strong flour which is rich in gluten, whether it is white or brown (this includes granary and stoneground) is best kept for bread and Yorkshire pudding. It is also recommended for steamed suet puddings as well as puff pastry. oo flour is designed for pasta making and there is no substitute for this flour. Ordinary flour or weak flour is best for cakes, biscuits and sauces – they absorb fats easily and give a soft, light texture. This flour comes in plain white or self-raising, as well as wholemeal varieties. Self-raising flour, which has the raising agent already incorporated, is best kept for sponge cakes where it is important that an even rise is achieved. Plain flour can be used for all types of baking and sauces. If using plain flour for scones or cakes and puddings, unless otherwise stated in the recipe, use

1 teaspoon of baking powder to 225 g/ 8 oz of plain flour. With sponge cakes and light fruit cakes, it is best to use self-raising flour as the raising agent has already been added to the flour. This way there is no danger of using too much, which can result in a sunken cake with a sour taste. There are other raising agents that are also used. Some cakes use bicarbonate of soda with or without cream of tartar, blended with warm or sour milk. Whisked eggs also act as a raising agent as the air trapped in the egg ensures that the mixture rises. Generally no other raising agent is required.

Flour also comes ready sifted. There is even a special sponge flour designed especially for whisked sponges. It is also possible to buy flours that cater for coeliacs which contain no gluten. Buckwheat, soya and chick pea flours are also available.

Eggs

When a recipe states 1 egg, it is generally accepted this refers to a medium egg. Over the past few years the grading of eggs has changed. For years, eggs were sold as small, standard and large, then this method changed and they were graded in numbers with 1 being the largest. The general feeling by the public was that this system was misleading, so now we buy our eggs as small, medium and large. Due to the slight risk of salmonella, all eggs are now sold date stamped to ensure that the eggs are used in their prime. This applies even to farm eggs which are no longer allowed to be sold straight from the farm. Look for the lion quality stamp (on 75% of all eggs sold) which guarantees that the eggs come from hens vaccinated against salmonella, have been laid in the UK and are produced to the highest food safety and standards. All of these eggs carry a best before date.

There are many types of eggs sold and it really is a question of personal preference which ones are chosen. All offer the same nutritional benefits. The majority of eggs sold in this country are caged eggs. These are the cheapest eggs and the hens have been fed on a manufactured mixed diet.

Barn eggs are from hens kept in barns who are free to roam within the barn. However, their diet is similar to caged hens and the barns may be overcrowded.

It is commonly thought that free-range eggs are from hens that lead a much more natural life and are fed natural foods. This, however, is not always the case and in some instances they may still live in a crowded environment.

Four-grain eggs are from hens that have been fed on grain and no preventative medicines have been included in their diet. Organic eggs are from hens that live in a flock, whose beaks are not clipped and who are completely free to roam. Obviously, these eggs are much more expensive than the others.

Store eggs in the refrigerator with the round end uppermost (as packed in the egg boxes). Allow to come to room temperature before using. Do remember, raw or semi-cooked eggs should not be given to babies, toddlers, pregnant women, the elderly and those suffering from a reccurring illness.

Sugar

Sugar not only offers taste to baking but also adds texture and volume to the mixture. It is generally accepted that caster sugar is best for sponge cakes, puddings and meringues. Its fine granules disperse evenly when creaming or whisking. Granulated sugar is used for more general cooking, such as stewing fruit, whereas demerara sugar with its toffee taste and crunchy texture is good for sticky puddings and cakes such as flapjacks. For rich fruit cakes, Christmas puddings and cakes, use the muscovado sugars, which give a rich intense molasses or treacle flavour.

Icing sugar is used primarily for icings but can also be used in meringues and in fruit sauces when the sugar needs to dissolve quickly. You could also try flavouring your own sugar. Place a vanilla pod in a screw top jar, fill with caster sugar, screw down the lid and leave for 2–3 weeks before using. Top up after use or use thinly pared lemon or orange rind in the same manner.

If trying to reduce sugar intake then use the unrefined varieties, such as golden granulated, golden caster, unrefined demerara and the muscovado sugars. All of these are a little sweeter than their refined counterparts, so less is required. Alternatively, clear honey or fructose (fruit sugar) can reduce sugar intake as they have similar calories to sugar, but are twice as sweet. Also, they have a slow release so their effect lasts longer. Dried fruits can also be included in the diet to top up sugar intake.

Yeast

There is something very comforting about the aroma of freshly baked bread, and the taste is far different and superior to commercially made bread. Bread making is regarded by some as being a time consuming process, but with the advent of fast-acting yeast this no longer applies. There are three types of yeast available: fresh yeast,

which can now be bought in the instore bakery department of many supermarkets (fresh yeast freezes well); dried yeast, which is available in tins; and quick-acting yeast which comes in packets.

Fresh yeast should be bought in small quantities; it has a putty-like colour and texture with a slight wine smell. It should be creamed with a little sugar and some warm liquid before being added to the flour. Dried yeast can be stored for up to six months and comes in small hard granules. It should be sprinkled on to warm liquid with a little sugar then left to stand, normally between 15–20 minutes, until the mixture froths. When replacing the fresh yeast with dried yeast, use 1 tablespoon of dried yeast for 25 g/1 oz of fresh yeast.

Quick acting yeast cuts down the time of bread making and eliminates the need for proving the bread twice. Also, the yeast can be added straight to the flour without it needing to be activated. When replacing quick-acting yeast for dried yeast, you will need double the amount.

When using yeast, the most important thing to remember is that yeast is a living plant and needs food, water and warmth to work.

Equipment

Nowadays, you can get lost in the cookware sections of some of the larger stores – they really are a cook's paradise with gadgets, cooking tools and state-of-the-art electronic devices. A few, well-picked, high quality utensils and pieces of equipment will be frequently used and will therefore be a much wiser buy than cheaper gadgets.

Cooking equipment not only assists in the kitchen, but can make all the difference between success and failure. Take the humble cake tin: although a very basic piece of cooking equipment, it plays an essential role in baking. Using the incorrect size can be a disaster, as a tin that is too large will spread the mixture too thinly and the result will be a flat, limp-looking cake. On the other hand, cramming the mixture into a tin which is too small will result in the mixture rising up and out of the tin.

Baking Equipment

To ensure successful baking it is worth investing in a selection of high quality tins, which if looked after properly should last for many years. Follow the manufacturer's instructions when first using and ensure that the tins are thoroughly washed and dried after use and before putting away. Perhaps the most useful of tins for

baking are sandwich cake tins, ideal for classics such as Victoria sponge, genoese and coffee and walnut cake. You will need two tins and they are normally 18 cm/7 inches or 20.5 cm/ 8 inches in diameter, about 5–7.5cm/ 2–3 inches deep, and are often non-stick.

With deep cake tins, it is personal choice whether you buy round or square tins, and they vary in size from 12.5–35.5 cm/5–14 inches with a depth of between 12.5–15 cm/5–6 inches. A deep cake tin, for everyday fruit or Madeira cake is a must – a useful size is 20.5 cm/8 inches.

Loaf tins are used for bread, fruit or tea bread and terrines and normally come in two sizes, 450 g/1 lb and 900 g/2 lb.

Good baking sheets are a must for all cooks. Dishes that are too hot to handle such as apple pies should be placed directly on to a baking tray. Meringues, biscuits and cookies are also cooked on a baking tray. Do not confuse these with Swiss roll tins which have sides all around: a sheet only has one raised side.

Square or oblong shallow baking tins are also very useful for making tray bakes, fudge brownies, flapjacks and shortbread.

Patty tins are ideal for making small buns, jam tarts or mince pies, while

individual Yorkshire pudding tins and muffin tins or flan tins are also useful. They are available in a variety of sizes.

There are plenty of other tins to choose from, ranging from themed tins, such as Christmas tree shapes and numbers from 1–9, as well as tins shaped as petals, ring mould tins, (tins with a hole in the centre) and spring-form tins where the sides release after cooking allowing the finished cake to be removed easily.

Three to four different sizes of mixing bowls are also very useful.

Another piece of equipment which is worth having is a wire cooling rack. It is essential when baking to allow biscuits and cakes to cool after being removed from their tins.

A selection of different-sized roasting tins are also a worthwhile investment as they can double up as a bain marie, or for cooking larger quantities of cakes such as gingerbread. A few different tins and dishes are required if baking crumbles, soufflés and pies. Ramekin dishes and small pudding basins can be used for a variety of different recipes, as can small tartlet tins and dariole moulds. When purchasing your implements for baking, perhaps the rolling pin is one of the most important. Ideally it should be long and thin, heavy enough to roll the pastry out easily but not too heavy that it is uncomfortable to use. Pastry needs to be rolled out on a flat surface, and although a lightly floured flat surface will do, a marble slab will keep the pastry cool and ensure that the fats do not melt while being rolled. This helps to keep the pastry light, crisp and flaky rather than heavy and stodgy, which happens if the fat melts before being baked.

Other useful basic pastry implements are tools such as a pastry brush (which can be used to wet pastry or brush on a glaze), a pastry wheel for cutting and a sieve to remove impurities and also to sift air into the flour, encouraging the pastry or mixture to be lighter in texture.

Basic mixing cutlery is also essential, such as a wooden spoon (for mixing and creaming), a spatula (for transferring the mixture from the mixing bowl to the baking tins and spreading the mixture once it is in the tins) and a palette knife (to ease cakes and breads out of their tins before placing them on the wire racks to cool). Measuring spoons and cups are essential for accurate measuring of both dry and wet ingredients.

Electrical Equipment

Nowadays help from time-saving gadgets and electrical equipment make baking far more easy and quick. Equipment can be used for creaming, mixing, beating, whisking, kneading, grating and chopping. There is a wide choice of machines available from the most basic to the very sophisticated.

Food Processors

When choosing a machine, you must first decide what you need your processor to do. If you are a novice to baking, it may be a waste to start with a machine that offers a wide range of implements and functions. This can be off-putting and result in not using the machine to its full capabilities.

In general, while styling and product design play a role in the price, the more you pay, the larger the machine will be, with a bigger bowl capacity and many more gadgets attached. Nowadays, you can chop, shred, slice, chip, blend, purée, knead, whisk and cream anything. However, just what basic features should you ensure your machine has before buying it?

When buying a food processor look for measurements on the side of the processor bowl and machines with a removable feed tube which allows food or liquid to be added while the motor is still running. Look out for machines that have the facility to increase the capacity of the bowl (ideal when making soup) and have a pulse button for controlled chopping.

For many, storage is also an issue, so reversible discs and flex storage, or on more advanced models, a blade storage compartment or box, can be advantageous.

It is also worth thinking about machines that offer optional extras that can be bought as your cooking requirements change. For instance, mini chopping bowls are available for those wanting to chop small quantities of food. If time is an issue, dishwasher-friendly attachments may be vital. Citrus presses, liquidisers and whisks may all be useful attachments for the individual cook.

Blenders

Blenders often come as attachments to food processors and are generally used for liquidising and puréeing foods. There are two main types of blender. The first is known as a goblet blender. The blades of this blender are at the bottom of the goblet with measurements up the sides. The second blender is portable. It is hand-held and should be placed in a bowl to blend.

Food Mixers

These are ideally suited to mixing cakes and kneading dough, either as a table-top mixer or a hand-held mixer. Both are extremely useful and based on the same principle of mixing or whisking in an open bowl to allow more air to get to the mixture and therefore give a lighter texture.

The table-top mixers are freestanding and are capable of dealing with fairly large quantities of mixture. They are robust machines, capable of easily dealing with kneading dough and heavy cake mixing as well as whipping cream, whisking egg whites or making one-stage cakes. These mixers also offer a wide range of attachments ranging from liquidisers, mincers, juicers, can openers and many more and varied attachments.

Hand-held mixers are smaller than freestanding mixers and often come with their own bowl and stand from which they can be lifted off and used as hand-held devices. They have a motorised head with detachable twin whisks. These mixers are particularly versatile as they do not need a specific bowl in which to whisk. Any suitable mixing bowl can be used.

Basic Techniques

There is no mystery to successful baking, it really is easy providing you follow a few simple rules and guidelines. First, read the recipe right through before commencing. There is nothing more annoying than getting to the middle of a recipe and discovering that you are minus one or two of the ingredients. Until you are confident with a recipe do not try any short cuts, or you may find that you have left out a vital step which means that the recipe cannot work. Most of all, have patience, baking is easy – if you can read, you can bake.

Pastry Making

Pastry needs to be kept as cool as possible throughout. Cool hands help, but are not essential. Use cold or iced water, but not too much as pastry does not need to be wet. Make sure that your fat is not runny or melted but firm (this is why block fat is the best). Avoid using too much flour when rolling out as this alters the proportions, and also avoid handling the dough too much. Roll in one direction as this helps to ensure that the pastry does not shrink. Allow the pastry to rest after rolling, preferably in the refrigerator. If you follow these guidelines but still your pastry is not as good as you would like it to be, then make it in a processor instead.

Lining a Flan Case

It is important to choose the right tin to bake with. You will often find that a loose-bottomed metal flan case is the best option as it conducts heat more efficiently and evenly than a ceramic dish. It also has the added advantage of a removable base, which makes the transfer of the final flan or tart a much simpler process; it simply lifts out, keeping the pastry intact.

Roll the pastry out on a lightly floured surface ensuring that it is a few inches larger than the flan case. Wrap the pastry around the rolling pin, lift and place in the tin. Carefully ease the pastry into the base and sides of the tin, ensuring that there are no gaps or tears in the pastry. Allow to rest for a few minutes then trim the edge either with a sharp knife or by rolling a rolling pin across the top of the flan tin.

Baking Blind

The term baking blind means that the pastry case needs to be cooked without the filling, resulting in a crisp pastry shell that is either partially or fully cooked depending on whether the filling needs any cooking. Pastry shells can be prepared ahead of time, as they last for several days if stored correctly in an airtight container or longer if frozen.

To bake blind, line a pastry case with the prepared pastry and allow to rest in the refrigerator for 30 minutes. This will help to minimise shrinkage while it is being cooked. Remove from the refrigerator and lightly prick the base all over with a fork (do not do this if the filling is runny). Brush with a little beaten egg if desired or simply line the case with a large square of greaseproof paper, big enough to cover both the base and sides of the pastry case. Fill with either ceramic baking beans or dried beans. Place on a baking sheet and bake in a preheated oven, generally at 200°C/400°F/Gas Mark 6, remembering that ovens can take at least 15 minutes to reach this heat. Cook for 10–12 minutes, then remove from the oven and discard the paper and beans. Return to the oven and continue to cook for a further 5–10 minutes depending on whether the filling needs cooking. As a rule, unless otherwise stated, individual pastry tartlet cases also benefit from baking blind.

Covering a Pie Dish

To cover a pie, roll out the pastry until it is about two inches larger than the circumference of the dish. Cut a 2.5 cm/1 inch strip from around the outside of the pastry and then moisten the edge of the pie dish you are using. Place the strip on the edge of the dish and brush with water or beaten egg. Generously fill the pie dish until the surface is slightly rounded. Using the rolling pin, lift the remaining pastry and cover the pie dish. Press together, then seal. Using a sharp knife, trim off any excess pastry from around the edges. Try to avoid brushing the edges of the pastry, especially puff pastry as this prevents the pastry rising evenly. Before placing in the oven make a small hole in the centre of the pie to allow the steam to escape.

The edges of the pie can be forked by pressing the back of a fork around the edge of the pie, or instead crimp by pinching the edge crust holding the thumb and index finger of your right hand against the edge while gently pushing with the index finger of your left hand. Other ways of finishing the pie are to knock up (achieved by gently pressing your index finger down on to the rim and, at the same time, tapping a knife horizontally along the edge giving it a flaky appearance), or fluting the edges by pressing your thumb down on the edge of the pastry while gently drawing back an all-purpose knife about 1 cm/½ inch and repeating around the rim. Experiment by putting leaves and berries made out of leftover pastry to finish off the pie, then brush the top of the pie with beaten egg.

Lining Cake Tins

If a recipe states that the tin needs lining, do not be tempted to ignore this. Rich fruit cakes and other cakes that take a long time to cook benefit from the tin being lined so that the edges and base do not burn or dry out. Greaseproof or baking parchment paper is ideal for this. It is a good idea to have the paper at least double thickness, or preferably 3–4 thicknesses. Sponge cakes and other cakes that are cooked in 30 minutes or less are also better if the bases are lined as it is far easier to remove them from the tin.

The best way to line a round or square tin is to lightly draw around the base and then cut just inside the markings so it sits easily inside the tin. Next, lightly oil the paper so it easily peels away from the cake. If the sides of the tin also need to be lined, then cut a strip of paper long enough for the tin. This can be measured by wrapping a piece of string around the rim of the tin. Once again, lightly oil the paper, push against the tin and oil once more as this will hold the paper to the sides of the tin. Steamed puddings usually need only a disc of greaseproof paper at the bottom of the dish as the sides come away easily.

Hints for Successful Baking

Ensure that the ingredients are accurately measured. A cake that has too much flour or insufficient egg will be dry and crumbly. Take care when measuring the raising agent if used, as too much will mean that the cake will rise too quickly and then sink. Insufficient raising agent means the cake will not rise in the first place.

Ensure that the oven is preheated to the correct temperature, remembering that it can take 10 minutes to reach 180°C/350°F/Gas Mark 4. You may find that an oven thermometer is a good investment. Cakes are best if cooked in the centre of the preheated oven. Do try to avoid the temptation of opening the oven door at the beginning of cooking as a draft can make the cake sink. If using a fan oven then refer to the manufacturer's instructions, as they normally cook 10–20° hotter than conventional ovens.

Check that the cake is thoroughly cooked by removing from the oven and inserting a clean skewer into the cake. Leave for 30 seconds and remove. If the skewer is completely clean then the cake is cooked; if there is a little mixture left on the skewer then return to the oven for a few minutes.

Other problems that you may encounter while cake making are insufficient creaming of the fat and sugar or a curdled creamed mixture (which will result in a densely textured and often fairly solid cake). Flour that has not been folded in carefully enough or has not been mixed with enough raising agent may also result in a fairly heavy consistency. It is very important to try to ensure that the correct size of tin is used as you may end up either with a flat, hard cake or one which has spilled over the edge of the tin. Another tip to be aware of (especially when cooking with fruit) is that if the consistency is too soft, the cake will not be able to support the fruit and it will sink to the bottom.

Finally, when you take your cake out of the oven, unless the recipe states that it should be left in the tin until cold, leave for a few minutes and then loosen the edges and turn out on to a wire rack to cool. Cakes that are left in the tin for too long, unless otherwise stated, tend to sink or slightly overcook.

When storing, make sure the cake is completely cold before placing it into an airtight tin or plastic container.

Culinary Terms Explained

Bain marie A French term, meaning water bath. A shallow tin, often a roasting tin, half-filled with water. Smaller dishes of food are then placed in it, allowing them to cook at lower temperatures without over-heating. This method is often used to cook custards and other egg dishes or to keep some dishes warm.

Baking blind The method often used for cooking the pastry case of flans and tarts before the filling is added. After lining the tin with the uncooked pastry it is then covered with a sheet of greaseproof or baking parchment paper and weighed down with either ceramic baking beans or dried beans and is baked in the oven as directed in the recipe.

Baking parchment paper Used for wrapping food to be cooked (*en papillote*) and for lining cake tins to prevent sticking.

Baking powder A raising agent that works by producing carbon dioxide as a consequence of a reaction caused by the acid and alkali ingredients that expand during the baking process. This causes breads and cakes to rise.

Beating The method by which air is introduced into a mixture using a fork, wooden spoon, whisk or electric mixer. Beating is also used as a method to soften ingredients.

Bicarbonate of soda This acts as a raising agent in baking when combined with liquid.

Binding Adding liquid or egg to bring a dry mixture together. Normally this entails using either a fork, spoon or your fingertips.

Blender An electric machine with rotating blades used mainly with soft and wet ingredients to purée and liquidise, although it can grind dry ingredients such as nuts and breadcrumbs.

Blending Dry ingredients are mixed with liquid to form a smooth paste before a boiling liquid is added. Used for thickening stews, casseroles, soups and sauces.

Brioche A traditional bread eaten in France for breakfast, usually served warm. Brioche has a rich, bread-like texture containing yeast and is baked in the shape of a small cottage loaf. A delicious substitute for bread in bread and butter pudding.

Caramel Obtained by heating sugar at a very low heat until it turns liquid and deep brown in colour. This is used in dishes such as crème caramel, which is baked in a bain marie.

Centigrade This is a scale for measuring the temperature within the oven (also known as celcius).

Choux A type of pastry (rather like a glossy batter) that is piped into small balls on to a baking tray and baked until light and airy. They can then be filled with cream or savoury fillings.

Cocotte Another name for a ramekin, a small, ovenproof earthenware pot used for individual portions.

Cornstarch An American term for cornflour which is used to thicken consistency and can also be used in meringue-making to prevent the meringue becoming hard and brittle and to enhance its chewiness.

Cream of tartar Another raising agent often present in both self-raising flour and baking powder.

Creaming The method by which fat and sugar are beaten together until lighter in colour and fluffy. By creaming the fat in cake mixtures, air is incorporated into the fairly high fat content. It thus lightens the texture of cakes and puddings.

Crimping The fluted effect used for the decoration on pies or tarts created by pinching the edge crust while holding the thumb and index finger of your right hand against the edge and gently pushing with the index finger of your left hand.

Crumb The term by which flour and fat are combined typically for use in pastry, crumble and biscuits.

Curdle When the milk separates from a sauce through acidity or excessive heat. This can also happen to creamed cake mixtures that have separated due to the eggs being too cold or being added too quickly.

Dariole A small narrow mould with slopping sides used for making madeleines. Darioles can also be used for individual steamed or baked puddings and jellies.

Dough A dense mixture of flour, water and often yeast. Also used to describe raw pastry, scones and biscuit mixtures.

Dredging The sprinkling of food with a coating (generally of flour or sugar).

A board may be dredged with flour before the pastry is rolled out and cakes and biscuits can be dredged with sugar or icing sugar after baking.

Dropping consistency The consistency a cake or pudding mixture reaches before being cooked. It tends to be fairly soft (but not runny) and should drop off a spoon in around five seconds when tapped lightly on the side of a bowl.

Dust To sprinkle lightly, often with flour, sugar or icing sugar.

En croute Used to describe food which is covered with raw pastry and then baked.

En papillote A French term used to describe food which is baked, but is wrapped in greaseproof or baking parchment paper before cooking. This works well with fish as the aroma from the different herbs or spices and the fish are contained during cooking and not released until the paper parcel is opened.

Fermenting A term used during bread, beer or wine making to note the chemical change brought about through the use of a fermenting agent, such as yeast.

Filo A type of pastry that is wafer-thin. Three to four sheets are usually used at a time in baking.

Folding A method of combining creamed fat and sugar with flour in cake and pudding mixes usually by carefully mixing with a large metal spoon, either by cutting and folding, or by doing a figure of eight in order to maintain a light texture.

Glacé A French term meaning glossy or iced. Glacé icing is a quick icing often used to decorate cakes and biscuits. It is made using icing sugar and warm water.

Greaseproof paper Paper that tends to be relatively non-stick and which is used to line tins to prevent cakes and puddings from sticking.

Grinding Reducing hard ingredients such as nuts to crumbs, normally by the use of a grinder or a pestle and mortar.

Knead The process of pummelling and working dough in order to strengthen the gluten in the flour and make the dough more elastic, thus giving a good rise. Also applies to pastry making; the dough is kneaded on a lightly floured surface to give a smooth and elastic pastry, making it easier to roll and ensuring an even texture after baking. In both cases the outside of the dough is drawn into the centre.

Knock back The term used for a second kneading after the dough has been allowed to rise. This is done to ensure an even texture and to disperse any large pockets of air.

Pasteurising The term given when milk and eggs are heated to destroy bacteria.

Piping The way in which cakes and desserts are decorated, or the method by which choux pastry is placed on to a baking sheet. This is achieved by putting cream, icing or mixture in a nylon bag (with a nozzle attached) and then slowly forcing the filling through the nozzle and piping it on to the cake or baking tray.

Proving The term used in breadmaking when the bread is allowed to rise a second time after it has been kneaded once and then shaped before it is baked.

Puff pastry Probably the richest of pastries. When making from the beginning, it requires the lightest of handling.

Ramekin An ovenproof, earthenware dish which provides an individual serving.

Rice paper This edible paper is made from the pith of a Chinese tree and can be used as a base on which to bake sticky cakes and biscuits such as almond macaroons.

Rubbing in The method of combining fat into flour for crumble toppings, shortcrust pastry, biscuits and scones.

Scalloping The term given to a type of pie decoration achieved by horizontal cuts made in the pastry which is then pulled back with the knife to produce a scalloped effect.

Sifting The shaking of dry ingredients (primarily flour) through a metal or nylon sieve to remove impurities and introduce air before using in baking.

Unleavened Often refers to bread that does not use a raising agent and is therefore flat, such as Indian naan bread.

Vol-au-vent Translated it means to fly or float on the wind. This small and usually round or oval puff pastry case is first baked and then filled with savoury meat, seafood or vegetable filling in a sauce.

Whipping/whisking The term given to incorporating air rapidly into a mixture (either through using a manual whisk or an electric whisk).

Zest Very thin, long pieces of the coloured part of an orange, lemon or lime peel, containing the fruit oil which is responsible for the citrus flavour. Normally a zester is used which removes the zest without any of the bitter white pith. (Rind refers to the peel which has been grated on a grater into very small pieces.)

Apple & Cinnamon Crumble-top Cake

INGREDIENTS

Cuts into 8 slices

For the topping:

350 g/12 oz eating apples, peeled
1 tbsp lemon juice
125 g/4 oz self-raising flour
1 tsp ground cinnamon
75 g/3 oz butter or margarine
75 g/3 oz demerara sugar
1 tbsp milk

For the base:

125 g/4 oz butter or margarine
125 g/4 oz caster sugar
2 medium eggs
150 g/5 oz self-raising flour
Cream or freshly made custard,
   to serve

1 Preheat the oven to 180°C/350°F/Gas Mark 4, 10 minutes before baking. Lightly oil and line the base of a 20.5 cm/8 inch deep round cake tin with greaseproof or baking paper.

2 Finely chop the apples and mix with the lemon juice. Reserve while making the cake.

3 For the crumble topping, sift the flour and cinnamon together into a large bowl.

4 Rub the butter or margarine into the flour and cinnamon until the mixture resembles coarse breadcrumbs.

5 Stir the sugar into the breadcrumbs and reserve.

6 For the base, cream the butter or margarine and sugar together until light and fluffy. Gradually beat the eggs into the sugar and butter mixture a little at a time until all the egg has been added.

7 Sift the flour and gently fold in with a metal spoon or rubber spatula.

8 Spoon into the base of the prepared cake tin. Arrange the apple pieces on top, then lightly stir the milk into the crumble mixture.

9 Scatter the crumble mixture over the apples and bake in the preheated oven for 1½ hours. Serve cold with cream or custard.

TASTY TIP

For a crunchier-textured topping, stir in 50 g/2 oz of chopped mixed nuts and seeds to the crumble mixture in step 5.

2

6

9

Chocolate & Coconut Cake

INGREDIENTS

Cuts into 8 slices

125 g/4 oz plain dark chocolate,
   roughly chopped
175 g/6 oz butter or margarine
175 g/6 oz caster sugar
3 medium eggs, beaten
175 g/6 oz self-raising flour
1 tbsp cocoa powder
50 g/2 oz desiccated coconut

For the icing:

125 g/4 oz butter or margarine
2 tbsp creamed coconut
225 g/8 oz icing sugar
25 g/1 oz desiccated coconut,
   lightly toasted

TASTY TIP

Why not experiment with the chocolate in this recipe? For a different taste, try using orange-flavoured dark chocolate or add 1–2 tablespoons of rum when melting the chocolate.

1 Preheat the oven to 180°C/350°F/Gas Mark 4, 10 minutes before baking. Melt the chocolate in a small bowl placed over a saucepan of gently simmering water, ensuring that the base of the bowl does not touch the water. When the chocolate has melted, stir until smooth and allow to cool.

2 Lightly oil and line the bases of 2 x 18 cm/7 inch sandwich tins with greaseproof or baking paper. In a large bowl beat the butter or margarine and sugar together with a wooden spoon until light and creamy. Beat in the eggs a little at a time, then stir in the melted chocolate.

3 Sift the flour and cocoa powder together and gently fold into the chocolate mixture with a metal spoon or rubber spatula. Add the desiccated coconut and mix lightly. Divide between the 2 prepared tins and smooth the tops.

4 Bake in the preheated oven for 25–30 minutes, or until a skewer comes out clean when inserted into the centre of the cake. Allow to cool in the tin for 5 minutes, then turn out, discard the lining paper and leave on a wire rack until cold.

5 Beat together the butter or margarine and creamed coconut until light. Add the icing sugar and mix well. Spread half of the icing on 1 cake and press the cakes together. Spread the remaining icing over the top, sprinkle with the coconut and serve.

1

4

5

Citrus Cake

INGREDIENTS

Cuts into 6 slices

175 g/6 oz golden caster sugar

175 g/6 oz butter or margarine

3 medium eggs

2 tbsp orange juice

175 g/6 oz self-raising flour

finely grated rind of 2 oranges

5 tbsp lemon curd

125 g/4 oz icing sugar

finely grated rind of 1 lemon

1 tbsp freshly squeezed
  lemon juice

FOOD FACT

Repeated sifting as in step 3 removes impurities from the flour while adding air to it. Using golden caster sugar gives a richer sweeter taste than normal caster sugar and contrasts particularly well with the citrus flavours in this cake.

1 Preheat the oven to 325°C/170°F/Gas Mark 3, 10 minutes before baking. Lightly oil and line the base of a round 20.5 cm/8 inch deep cake tin with baking paper.

2 In a large bowl, cream the sugar and butter or margarine together until light and fluffy. Whisk the eggs together and beat into the creamed mixture a little at a time.

3 Beat in the orange juice with 1 tablespoon of the flour. Sift the remaining flour on to a large plate several times, then with a metal spoon or rubber spatula, fold into the creamed mixture.

4 Spoon into the prepared cake tin. Stir the finely grated orange rind into the lemon curd and dot randomly across the top of the mixture.

5 Using a fine skewer swirl the lemon curd through the cake mixture. Bake in the preheated oven for 35 minutes, until risen and golden. Allow to cool for 5 minutes in the tin, then turn out carefully on to a wire rack.

6 Sift the icing sugar into a bowl, add the grated lemon rind and juice and stir well to mix. When the cake is cold cover the top with the icing and serve.

2

4

5

Victoria Sponge with Mango & Mascarpone

INGREDIENTS

Cuts into 8 slices

175 g/6 oz caster sugar, plus extra
   for dusting
175 g/6 oz self-raising flour, plus extra
   for dusting
175 g/6 oz butter or margarine
3 large eggs
1 tsp vanilla essence
25 g/1 oz icing sugar
250 g/9 oz mascarpone cheese
1 large ripe mango, peeled

TASTY TIP

Mango has been used in this recipe, but 125 g/4 oz of mashed strawberries could be used instead. Reserve a few whole strawberries, slice and use to decorate the cake.

1 Preheat the oven to 190°C/375°F/Gas Mark 5, 10 minutes before baking. Lightly oil 2 x 18 cm/7 inch sandwich tins and lightly dust with caster sugar and flour, tapping the tins to remove any excess.

2 In a large bowl cream the butter or margarine and sugar together with a wooden spoon until light and creamy.

3 In another bowl mix the eggs and vanilla essence together. Sift the flour several times on to a plate.

4 Beat a little egg into the butter and sugar, then a little flour and beat well.

5 Continue adding the flour and eggs alternately, beating between each addition, until the mixture is well mixed and smooth. Divide the mixture between the 2 prepared cake tins, level the surface, then using the back of a large spoon, make a slight dip in the centre of each cake.

6 Bake in the preheated oven for 25–30 minutes, until the centre of the cake springs back when gently pressed with a clean finger. Turn out on to a wire rack and leave the cakes until cold.

7 Beat the icing sugar and mascarpone cheese together, then chop the mango into small cubes.

8 Use half the mascarpone and mango to sandwich the cakes together. Spread the rest of the mascarpone on top, decorate with the remaining mango and serve. Otherwise lightly cover and store in the refrigerator. Use within 3–4 days.

1

5

6

Almond Cake

INGREDIENTS

Cuts into 8 slices

225 g/8 oz butter or margarine

225 g/8 oz caster sugar

3 large eggs

1 tsp vanilla essence

1 tsp almond essence

125 g/4 oz self-raising flour

175 g/6 oz ground almonds

50 g/2 oz whole
   almonds, blanched

25 g/1 oz plain dark chocolate

TASTY TIP

Baking with ground almonds helps to keep the cake moist as well as adding a slightly nutty flavour to the cake. 1–2 tablespoons of orange water can be added with the zest of 1 orange in step 4 if a fragrant citrus flavour is desired, but do omit the vanilla essence.

1   Preheat the oven to 150°C/300°F/Gas Mark 2. Lightly oil and line the base of a 20.5 cm/8 inch deep round cake tin with greaseproof or baking paper.

2   Cream together the butter or margarine and sugar with a wooden spoon until light and fluffy.

3   Beat the eggs and essences together. Gradually add to the sugar and butter mixture and mix well between each addition.

4   Sift the flour and mix with the ground almonds. Beat into the egg mixture until mixed well and smooth. Pour into the prepared cake tin.

5   Roughly chop the whole almonds and scatter over the cake before baking in the preheated oven.

6   Bake in the preheated oven for 45 minutes, or until golden and risen and a skewer inserted into the centre of the cake comes out clean.

7   Remove from the tin and leave to cool on a wire rack. Melt the chocolate in a small bowl placed over a saucepan of gently simmering water, stirring until smooth and free of lumps.

8   Drizzle the melted chocolate over the cooled cake and serve once the chocolate has set.

2

5

8

Lemon Drizzle Cake

INGREDIENTS

Cuts into 16 squares

125 g/4 oz butter or margarine
175 g/6 oz caster sugar
2 large eggs
175 g/6 oz self-raising flour
2 lemons, preferably unwaxed
50 g/2 oz granulated sugar

FOOD FACT

This classic cake is a favourite in many kitchens. The buttery sponge is perfectly complimented by the lemon syrup, which soaks into the cake giving it a gooeyness which is even better the next day!

1 Preheat the oven to 180°C/350°F/Gas Mark 4, 10 minutes before baking. Lightly oil and line the base of an 18 cm/7 inch square cake tin with baking paper.

2 In a large bowl, cream the butter or margarine and sugar together until soft and fluffy.

3 Beat the eggs, then gradually add a little of the egg to the creamed mixture, adding 1 tablespoon of flour after each addition.

4 Finely grate the rind from 1 of the lemons and stir into the creamed mixture, beating well until smooth. Squeeze the juice from the lemon, strain, then stir into the mixture.

5 Spoon into the prepared tin, level the surface and bake in the preheated oven for 25–30 minutes. Using a zester remove the peel from the last lemon and mix with 25 g/1 oz of the granulated sugar and reserve.

6 Squeeze the juice into a small saucepan. Add the rest of the granulated sugar to the lemon juice in the saucepan and heat gently, stirring occasionally.

7 When the sugar has dissolved simmer gently for 3–4 minutes until syrupy.

8 With a cocktail stick or fine skewer prick the cake all over.

9 Sprinkle the lemon zest and sugar over the top of the cake, drizzle over the syrup and leave to cool in the tin. Cut the cake into squares and serve.

3

5

9

Double Chocolate Cake with Cinnamon

INGREDIENTS

Cuts into 10 slices

50 g/2 oz cocoa powder
1 tsp ground cinnamon
225 g/8 oz self-raising flour
225 g/8 oz unsalted butter
  or margarine
225 g/8 oz caster sugar
4 large eggs

For the filling:

125 g/4 oz white chocolate
50 ml/2 fl oz double cream
25 g/1 oz plain dark chocolate

HELPFUL HINT

Adding some sifted flour can help to prevent the mixture from curdling (see step 2). Removing the eggs from the refigerator and allowing them to return to room temperature before use also helps. Remember to add just a little egg at a time!

1 Preheat the oven to 190°C/375°F/Gas Mark 5, 10 minutes before baking. Lightly oil and line the base of 2 x 20.5 cm/8 inch sandwich tins with greaseproof or baking paper. Sift the cocoa powder, cinnamon and flour together and reserve.

2 In a large bowl cream the butter or margarine and sugar, until light and fluffy. Beat in the eggs a little at a time until they are all incorporated and the mixture is smooth. (If it looks curdled at any point beat in 1 tablespoon of the sifted flour.)

3 Using a rubber spatula or metal spoon, fold the sifted flour and cocoa powder into the egg mixture until mixed well.

4 Divide between the 2 prepared cake tins, and level the surface. Bake in the preheated oven for 25–30 minutes, until springy to the touch and a skewer inserted into the centre of the cake comes out clean. Turn out on to a wire rack to cool.

5 To make the filling, coarsely break the white chocolate and heat the cream very gently in a small saucepan. Add the broken chocolate, stirring until melted. Leave to cool, then using half of the cooled white chocolate sandwich the cakes together.

6 Top the cake with the remaining cooled white chocolate. Coarsely grate the dark chocolate over the top and serve.

3

5

6

Swiss Roll

INGREDIENTS

Cuts into 8 slices

75 g/3 oz self-raising flour

3 large eggs

1 tsp vanilla essence

90 g/3½ oz caster sugar

25 g/1 oz hazelnuts, toasted and
  finely chopped

3 tbsp apricot conserve

300 ml/½ pint double cream,
  lightly whipped

TASTY TIP

Any flavour of jam can be used in this recipe. While apricot jam is delicious, traditional raspberry or blackcurrant jam also works very well. In place of the cream why not try butter cream icing or beaten mascarpone as a filling.

1 Preheat the oven to 220°C/425°F/Gas Mark 7, 15 minutes before baking. Lightly oil and line the base of a 23 x 33 cm/9 x 13 inch Swiss roll tin with a single sheet of greaseproof or baking paper.

2 Sift the flour several times, then reserve on top of the oven to warm a little.

3 Place a mixing bowl with the eggs, vanilla essence and sugar over a pan of hot water, ensuring that the bowl is not touching the water.

4 With the saucepan off the heat whisk with an electric hand whisk until the egg mixture becomes pale and mousse-like and has increased in volume.

5 Remove the basin from the saucepan and continue to whisk for a further 2–3 minutes. Sift in the flour and very gently fold in using a metal spoon or rubber spatula, trying not to knock out the air whisked in already. Pour into the prepared tin tilting to ensure that the mixture is evenly distributed. Bake in the preheated oven for 10–12 minutes, or until well risen, golden brown and the top springs back when lightly touched.

6 Sprinkle the toasted, chopped hazelnuts over a large sheet of greaseproof paper.

7 When the cake has cooked turn out on to the hazelnut covered paper and trim the edges of the cake. Holding an edge of the paper with the short side of the cake nearest you, roll the cake up.

8 When fully cold carefully unroll and spread with the jam and then the cream. Roll back up and serve. Otherwise, store in the refrigerator and eat within 2 days.

4

7

8

Toffee Apple Cake

INGREDIENTS

Cuts into 8 slices

2 small eating apples, peeled

4 tbsp soft dark brown sugar

175 g/6 oz butter or margarine

175 g/6 oz caster sugar

3 medium eggs

175 g/6 oz self-raising flour

150 ml/¼ pint double cream

2 tbsp icing sugar

½ tsp vanilla essence

½ tsp ground cinnamon

TASTY TIP

The dark brown sugar used in this recipe could be replaced with a dark muscovado sugar to give a deliciously rich toffee flavour to the apples. When baked the sugar will melt slightly into a caramel consistency.

1   Preheat the oven to 180°C/350°F/Gas Mark 4, 10 minutes before baking time. Lightly oil and line the bases of 2 x 20.5 cm/8 inch sandwich tins with greaseproof or baking paper.

2   Thinly slice the apples and toss in the brown sugar until well coated. Arrange them over the base of the prepared tins and reserve.

3   Cream together the butter or margarine and caster sugar until light and fluffy.

4   Beat the eggs together in a small bowl and gradually beat them into the creamed mixture, beating well between each addition.

5   Sift the flour into the mixture and using a metal spoon or rubber spatula, fold in.

6   Divide the mixture between the 2 cake tins and level the surface.

7   Bake in the preheated oven for 25–30 minutes, until golden and well risen. Leave in the tins to cool.

8   Lightly whip the cream with 1 tablespoon of the icing sugar and the vanilla essence.

9   Sandwich the cakes together with the cream. Mix the remaining icing sugar and ground cinnamon together, sprinkle over the top of the cake and serve.

2

4

9

Cappuccino Cakes

INGREDIENTS

Makes 6

125 g/4 oz butter or margarine
125 g/4 oz caster sugar
2 medium eggs
1 tbsp strong black coffee
150 g/5 oz self-raising flour
125 g/4 oz mascarpone cheese
1 tbsp icing sugar, sifted
1 tsp vanilla essence
sifted cocoa powder, to dust

TASTY TIP

The combination of coffee with the vanilla-flavoured mascarpone is heavenly! Make sure, however, that you use a good-quality coffee in this recipe. Colombian coffee is generally good and at its best possesses a smooth rounded flavour.

1 Preheat the oven to 190°C/375°F/Gas Mark 5, 10 minutes before baking. Place 6 large paper muffin cases into a muffin tin or alternatively place on to a baking sheet.

2 Cream the butter or margarine and sugar together until light and fluffy. Break the eggs into a small bowl and beat lightly with a fork.

3 Using a wooden spoon beat the eggs into the butter and sugar mixture a little at a time, until they are all incorporated.

4 If the mixture looks curdled beat in a spoonful of the flour to return the mixture to a smooth consistency. Finally beat in the black coffee.

5 Sift the flour into the mixture, then with a metal spoon or rubber spatula gently fold in the flour.

6 Place spoonfuls of the mixture into the muffin cases.

7 Bake in the preheated oven for 20–25 minutes, or until risen and springy to the touch. Cool on a wire rack.

8 In a small bowl beat together the mascarpone cheese, icing sugar and vanilla essence.

9 When the cakes are cold, spoon the vanilla mascarpone on to the top of each one. Dust with cocoa powder and serve. Store in the refrigerator and eat within 24 hours.

4

6

9

Honey Cake

INGREDIENTS

Cuts into 6 slices

50 g/2 oz butter
25 g/1 oz caster sugar
125 g/4 oz clear honey
175 g/6 oz plain flour
½ tsp bicarbonate of soda
½ tsp mixed spice
1 medium egg
2 tbsp milk
25 g/1 oz flaked almonds
1 tbsp clear honey, to drizzle

TASTY TIP

Serve a slice of this cake with a large spoonful of Greek yogurt on the side. The tart taste of the yogurt compliments the sweetness of the honey and spice perfectly – ideal for an afternoon treat.

1 Preheat the oven to 180°C/350°F/Gas Mark 4, 10 minutes before baking. Lightly oil and line the base of an 18 cm/7 inch deep round cake tin with lightly oiled greaseproof or baking paper.

2 In a saucepan gently heat the butter, sugar and honey until the butter has just melted.

3 Sift the flour, bicarbonate of soda and mixed spice together into a bowl.

4 Beat the egg and the milk until mixed thoroughly.

5 Make a well in the centre of the sifted flour and pour in the melted butter and honey.

6 Using a wooden spoon, beat well, gradually drawing in the flour from the sides of the bowl.

7 When all the flour has been beaten in, add the egg mixture and mix thoroughly. Pour into the prepared tin and sprinkle with the flaked almonds.

8 Bake in the preheated oven for 30–35 minutes, or until well risen and golden brown and a skewer inserted into the centre of the cake comes out clean.

9 Remove from the oven, cool for a few minutes in the tin before turning out and leaving to cool on a wire rack. Drizzle with the remaining tablespoon of honey and serve.

2

5

7

Fruit Cake

INGREDIENTS

Cuts into 10 slices

225 g/8 oz butter or margarine

200 g/7 oz soft brown sugar

finely grated rind of 1 orange

1 tbsp black treacle

3 large eggs, beaten

275 g/10 oz plain flour

¼ tsp ground cinnamon

½ tsp mixed spice

pinch of freshly grated nutmeg

¼ tsp bicarbonate of soda

75 g/3 oz mixed peel

50 g/2 oz glacé cherries

125 g/4 oz raisins

125 g/4 oz sultanas

125 g/4 oz ready-to-eat dried
  apricots, chopped

TASTY TIP

For a fruit cake with a kick, remove the cake from the oven when cooked and leave to cool. When the cake has cooled, turn out and make holes in the base of the cake with a skewer. Dribble over 4–5 tablespoons of your favourite alcohol such as whisky, brandy or Drambuie.

1 Preheat the oven to 150°C/300°C/Gas Mark 2, 10 minutes before baking. Lightly oil and line a 23 cm/9 inch deep round cake tin with a double thickness of greaseproof paper.

2 In a large bowl cream together the butter or margarine, sugar and orange rind, until light and fluffy, then beat in the treacle.

3 Beat in the eggs a little at a time, beating well between each addition.

4 Reserve 1 tablespoon of the flour. Sift the remaining flour, the spices and bicarbonate of soda into the mixture.

5 Mix all the fruits and the reserved flour together, then stir into the cake mixture.

6 Turn into the prepared tin and smooth the top, making a small hollow in the centre of the cake mixture.

7 Bake in the preheated oven for 1 hour, then reduce the heat to 140°C/275°F/Gas Mark 1.

8 Bake for a further 1½ hours, or until cooked and a skewer inserted into the centre comes out clean. Leave to cool in the tin, then turn the cake out and serve. Otherwise, when cold store in an airtight tin.

2

5

6

Banana Cake

INGREDIENTS

Cuts into 8 slices

3 medium-sized ripe bananas
1 tsp lemon juice
150 g/5 oz soft brown sugar
75 g/3 oz butter or margarine
250 g/9 oz self-raising flour
1 tsp ground cinnamon
3 medium eggs
50 g/2 oz walnuts, chopped
1 tsp each ground cinnamon and
    caster sugar, to decorate
fresh cream, to serve

HELPFUL HINT

The riper the bananas used in this recipe the better! Look out for reductions in supermarkets and fruit shops as ripe bananas are often sold very cheaply. This cake tastes really delicious the day after it has been made – the sponge solidifies slightly yet does not lose any moisture. Eat within 3–4 days.

1 Preheat the oven to 190°C/375°F/Gas Mark 5, 10 minutes before baking. Lightly oil and line the base of an 18 cm/7 inch deep round cake tin with greaseproof or baking paper.

2 Mash 2 of the bananas in a small bowl, sprinkle with the lemon juice and a heaped tablespoon of the sugar. Mix together lightly and reserve.

3 Gently heat the remaining sugar and butter or margarine in a small saucepan until the butter has just melted.

4 Pour into a small bowl, then allow to cool slightly. Sift the flour and cinnamon into a large bowl and make a well in the centre.

5 Beat the eggs into the cooled sugar mixture, pour into the well of flour, and mix thoroughly.

6 Gently stir in the mashed banana mixture. Pour half of the mixture into the prepared tin. Thinly slice the remaining banana and arrange over the cake mixture.

7 Sprinkle over the chopped walnuts, then cover with the remaining cake mixture.

8 Bake in the preheated oven for 50–55 minutes, or until well risen and golden brown. Allow to cool in the tin, turn out and sprinkle with the ground cinnamon and caster sugar. Serve hot or cold with a jug of fresh cream for pouring.

2

5

7

Coffee & Pecan Cake

INGREDIENTS

Cuts into 8 slices

175 g/6 oz self-raising flour
125 g/4 oz butter or margarine
175 g/6 oz golden caster sugar
1 tbsp instant coffee powder
  or granules
2 large eggs
50 g/2 oz pecans,
  roughly chopped

For the icing:

1 tsp instant coffee powder
  or granules
1 tsp cocoa powder
75 g/3 oz unsalted
  butter, softened
175 g/6 oz icing sugar, sifted
whole pecans, to decorate

HELPFUL HINT

To enjoy this cake whenever you want, simply bake in bulk. Follow the recipe up to step 5, then when the cakes have cooled wrap in greaseproof paper or tinfoil and freeze. When desired, remove from the freezer and allow to defrost at room temperature. Serve with or without icing.

1   Preheat the oven to 190°C/375°F/Gas Mark 5, 10 minutes before baking. Lightly oil and line the bases of 2 x 18 cm/7 inch sandwich tins with greaseproof or baking paper. Sift the flour and reserve.

2   Beat the butter or margarine and sugar together until light and creamy. Dissolve the coffee in 2 tablespoons of hot water and allow to cool.

3   Lightly mix the eggs with the coffee liquid. Gradually beat into the creamed butter and sugar, adding a little of the sifted flour with each addition.

4   Fold in the pecans, then divide the mixture between the prepared tins and bake in the preheated oven for 20–25 minutes, or until well risen and firm to the touch.

5   Leave to cool in the tins for 5 minutes before turning out and cooling on a wire rack.

6   To make the icing, blend together the coffee and cocoa powder with enough boiling water to make a stiff paste. Beat into the butter and icing sugar.

7   Sandwich the 2 cakes together using half of the icing. Spread the remaining icing over the top of the cake and decorate with the whole pecans to serve. Store in an airtight tin.

3

4

6

Carrot Cake

INGREDIENTS

Cuts into 8 slices

200 g/7 oz plain flour

1/2 tsp ground cinnamon

1/2 tsp freshly grated nutmeg

1 tsp baking powder

1 tsp bicarbonate of soda

150 g/5 oz dark
  muscovado sugar

200 ml/7 fl oz vegetable oil

3 medium eggs

225 g/8 oz carrots, peeled and
  roughly grated

50 g/2 oz chopped walnuts

For the icing:

175 g/6 oz cream cheese

finely grated rind of 1 orange

1 tbsp orange juice

1 tsp vanilla essence

125 g/4 oz icing sugar

TASTY TIP

For a fruitier cake, add 1 grated apple and 50 g/2 oz of dried sultanas in step 5. To plump up the dried sultanas, soak for an hour, or overnight in 300 ml/ 1/2 pint of cold tea.

1 Preheat the oven to 150°C/300°F/Gas Mark 2, 10 minutes before baking. Lightly oil and line the base of a 15 cm/6 inch deep square cake tin with greaseproof or baking paper.

2 Sift the flour, spices, baking powder and bicarbonate of soda together into a large bowl.

3 Stir in the dark muscovado sugar and mix together.

4 Lightly whisk the oil and eggs together, then gradually stir into the flour and sugar mixture. Stir well.

5 Add the carrots and walnuts. Mix thoroughly, then pour into the prepared cake tin. Bake in the preheated oven for 1¼ hours, or until light and springy to the touch and a skewer inserted into the centre of the cake comes out clean.

6 Remove from the oven and allow to cool in the tin for 5 minutes before turning out on to a wire rack. Reserve until cold.

7 To make the icing, beat together the cream cheese, orange rind, orange juice and vanilla essence. Sift the icing sugar and stir into the cream cheese mixture.

8 When cold, discard the lining paper, spread the cream cheese icing over the top and serve cut into squares.

2

5

7

Whisked Sponge Cake

INGREDIENTS

Cuts into 6 slices

125 g/4 oz plain flour, plus 1 tsp

175 g/6 oz caster sugar,
   plus 1 tsp

3 medium eggs

1 tsp vanilla essence

4 tbsp raspberry jam

50 g/2 oz fresh
   raspberries, crushed

icing sugar, to dredge

1 Preheat the oven to 200°C/400°F/Gas Mark 6, 15 minutes before baking. Mix 1 teaspoon of the flour and 1 teaspoon of the sugar together. Lightly oil 2 x 18 cm/7 inch sandwich tins and dust lightly with the sugar and flour.

2 Place the eggs in a large heatproof bowl. Add the sugar, then place over a saucepan of gently simmering water ensuring that the base of the bowl does not touch the hot water. Using an electric whisk beat the sugar and eggs until they become light and fluffy. (The whisk should leave a trail in the mixture when it is lifted out.)

3 Remove the bowl from the saucepan of water, add the vanilla essence and continue beating for 2–3 minutes. Sift the flour gently into the egg mixture and using a metal spoon or rubber spatula carefully fold in, taking care not to over mix and remove all the air that has been whisked in.

4 Divide the mixture between the 2 prepared cake tins. Tap lightly on the work surface to remove any air bubbles. Bake in the preheated oven for 20–25 minutes, or until golden. Test that the cake is ready by gently pressing the centre with a clean finger – it should spring back.

5 Leave to cool in the tins for 5 minutes, then turn out on to a wire rack. Blend the jam and the crushed raspberries together. When the cakes are cold spread over the jam mixture and sandwich together. Dredge the top with icing sugar and serve.

TASTY TIP

For a creamier low-fat filling mix the crushed raspberries or strawberries with 4 tablespoons each of low-fat Greek yogurt and low-fat crème fraîche.

1

2

5

Marble Cake

INGREDIENTS

Cuts into 8 slices

225 g/8 oz butter or margarine
225 g/8 oz caster sugar
4 medium eggs
225 g/8 oz self-raising
  flour, sifted
finely grated rind and juice
  of 1 orange
25 g/1 oz cocoa powder, sifted

For the topping:
zest and juice of 1 orange
1 tbsp granulated sugar

HELPFUL HINT
This cake has a wonderful combination of rich chocolate and orangey sponge. It is important not to swirl too much in step 2, as the desired effect is to have blocks of different coloured sponge.

1   Preheat the oven to 190°C/375°F/Gas Mark 5, 10 minutes before baking. Lightly oil and line the base of an 20.5 cm/8 inch deep round cake tin with greaseproof or baking paper.

2   In a large bowl, cream the butter or margarine and sugar together until light and fluffy.

3   Beat the eggs together. Beat into the creamed mixture a little at a time, beating well between each addition. When all the egg has been added, fold in the flour with a metal spoon or rubber spatula.

4   Divide the mixture equally between 2 bowls. Beat the grated orange rind into one of the bowls with a little of the orange juice. Mix the cocoa powder with the remaining orange juice until smooth, then add to the other bowl and beat well.

5   Spoon the mixture into the prepared tin, in alternate spoonfuls. When all the cake mixture is in the tin, take a skewer and swirl it in the 2 mixtures.

6   Tap the base of the tin on the work surface to level the mixture. Bake in the preheated oven for 50 minutes, or until cooked and a skewer inserted into the centre of the cake comes out clean.

7   Remove from the oven and leave in the tin for a few minutes before cooling on a wire rack. Discard the lining paper.

8   For the topping, place the orange zest and juice with the granulated sugar in a small saucepan and heat gently until the sugar has dissolved. Bring to the boil and simmer gently for 3–4 minutes, until the juice is syrupy. Pour over the cooled cake and serve when cool. Otherwise, store in an airtight tin.

4

5

8

Rich Chocolate Cup Cakes

INGREDIENTS

Makes 12

175 g/6 oz self-raising flour
25 g/1 oz cocoa powder
175 g/6 oz soft light brown sugar
75 g/3 oz butter, melted
2 medium eggs, lightly beaten
1 tsp vanilla essence
40 g/1½ oz maraschino cherries,
  drained and chopped

For the chocolate icing:

50 g/2 oz plain dark chocolate
25 g/1 oz unsalted butter
25 g/1 oz icing sugar, sifted

For the cherry icing:

125 g/4 oz icing sugar
7 g/¼ oz unsalted butter, melted
1 tsp syrup from the maraschino
  cherries
3 maraschino cherries, halved,
  to decorate

TASTY TIP

The cakes should only come about three-quarters of the way up the cases and have flat tops to allow the thick icing to be spooned over.

1. Preheat the oven to 180°C/350°F/Gas Mark 4, 10 minutes before baking. Line a 12-hole muffin or deep bun tin tray with paper muffin cases. Sift the flour and cocoa powder into a bowl. Stir in the sugar, then add the melted butter, eggs and vanilla essence. Beat together with a wooden spoon for 3 minutes or until well blended.

2. Divide half the mixture between 6 of the paper cases. Dry the cherries thoroughly on absorbent kitchen paper, then fold into the remaining mixture and spoon into the rest of the paper cases.

3. Bake on the shelf above the centre of the preheated oven for 20 minutes, or until a skewer inserted into the centre of a cake comes out clean. Transfer to a wire rack and leave to cool.

4. For the chocolate icing, melt the chocolate and butter in a heatproof bowl set over a saucepan of hot water. Remove from the heat and leave to cool for 3 minutes, stirring occasionally. Stir in the icing sugar. Spoon over the 6 plain chocolate cakes and leave to set.

5. For the cherry icing, sift the icing sugar into a bowl and stir in 1 tablespoon of boiling water, the butter and cherry syrup. Spoon the icing over the remaining 6 cakes, decorate each with a halved cherry and leave to set.

1

3

4

Moist Mocha & Coconut Cake

INGREDIENTS

Makes 9 squares

3 tbsp ground coffee
5 tbsp hot milk
75 g/3 oz butter
175 g/6 oz golden syrup
25 g/1 oz soft light brown sugar
40 g/1½ oz desiccated coconut
150 g/5 oz plain flour
25 g/1 oz cocoa powder
½ tsp bicarbonate of soda
2 medium eggs, lightly beaten
2 chocolate flakes, to decorate

For the coffee icing:

225 g/8 oz icing sugar, sifted
125 g/4 oz butter, softened

1   Preheat the oven to 170°C/325°F/Gas Mark 3, 10 minutes before baking. Lightly oil and line a deep 20.5 cm/8 inch square tin with nonstick baking parchment. Place the ground coffee in a small bowl and pour over the hot milk. Leave to infuse for 5 minutes, then strain through a tea-strainer or a sieve lined with muslin. You will end up with about 4 tablespoons of liquid. Reserve.

2   Put the butter, golden syrup, sugar and coconut in a small heavy-based saucepan and heat gently until the butter has melted and the sugar dissolved. Sift the flour, cocoa powder and bicarbonate of soda together and stir into the melted mixture with the eggs and 3 tablespoons of the coffee-infused milk.

3   Pour the mixture into the prepared tin. Bake on the centre shelf of the preheated oven for 45 minutes, or until the cake is well risen and firm to the touch. Leave in the tin for 10 minutes to cool slightly, then turn out onto a wire rack to cool completely.

4   For the icing, gradually add the icing sugar to the softened butter and beat together until mixed. Add the remaining 1 tablespoon of coffee-infused milk and beat until light and fluffy.

5   Carefully spread the coffee icing over the top of the cake, then cut into 9 squares. Decorate each square with a small piece of chocolate flake and serve.

HELPFUL HINT

It is important to use a very fine strainer to remove as much of the coffee as possible or the cake will have an unpleasant gritty texture.

2

3

5

All-in-one Chocolate Fudge Cakes

INGREDIENTS

Makes 15 squares

175 g/6 oz soft dark brown sugar
175 g/6 oz butter, softened
150 g/5 oz self-raising flour
25 g/1 oz cocoa powder
½ tsp baking powder
pinch of salt
3 medium eggs, lightly beaten
1 tbsp golden syrup

For the fudge topping:
75 g/3 oz granulated sugar
150 ml/¼ pint evaporated milk
175 g/6 oz plain dark chocolate,
  roughly chopped
40 g/1½ oz unsalted butter, softened
125 g/4 oz soft fudge sweets,
  finely chopped

1 Preheat the oven to 180°C/350°F/Gas Mark 4, 10 minutes before baking. Oil and line a 28 x 18 x 2.5 cm/ 11 x 7 x 1 inch cake tin with nonstick baking parchment.

2 Place the soft brown sugar and butter in a bowl and sift in the flour, cocoa powder, baking powder and salt. Add the eggs and golden syrup, then beat with an electric whisk for 2 minutes, before adding 2 tablespoons of warm water and beating for a further 1 minute.

3 Turn the mixture into the prepared tin and level the top with the back of a spoon. Bake on the centre shelf of the preheated oven for 30 minutes, or until firm to the touch. Turn the cake out onto a wire rack and leave to cool before removing the baking parchment.

4 To make the topping, gently heat the sugar and evaporated milk in a saucepan, stirring frequently, until the sugar has dissolved. Bring the mixture to the boil and simmer for 6 minutes, without stirring.

5 Remove the mixture from the heat. Add the chocolate and butter and stir until melted and blended. Pour into a bowl and chill in the refrigerator for 1–2 hours or until thickened. Spread the topping over the cake, then sprinkle with the chopped fudge. Cut the cake into 15 squares before serving.

TASTY TIP
Use a mixture of fudge sweets for the topping on this cake, including chocolate, vanilla and toffee flavours.

2

3

5

Chocolate & Saffron Cheesecake

INGREDIENTS

Serves 6

¼ tsp saffron threads

175 g/6 oz plain flour

pinch of salt

75 g/3 oz butter

1 tbsp caster sugar

1 medium egg yolk

350 g/12 oz curd cheese

75 g/3 oz golden granulated sugar

125 g/4 oz plain dark chocolate,
   melted and cooled

6 tbsp milk

3 medium eggs

1 tbsp icing sugar, sifted,
   to decorate

FOOD FACT

Saffron is the stamen of a particular type of crocus. It must be picked by hand and the yield is very small, making it very expensive. However, it is always used very sparingly and keeps very well.

1 Preheat the oven to 200°C/400°F/Gas Mark 6, 15 minutes before baking. Lightly oil a 20.5 cm/8 inch fluted flan tin. Soak the saffron threads in 1 tablespoon of hot water for 20 minutes. Sift the flour and salt into a bowl. Cut the butter into small dice, then add to the flour and using your fingertips, rub in the butter until the mixture resembles breadcrumbs. Stir in the sugar.

2 Beat the egg yolk with 1 tablespoon of cold water, add to the mixture and mix together until a smooth and pliable dough is formed. Add a little extra water if necessary. Knead on a lightly floured surface until free from cracks, then wrap in clingfilm and chill in the refrigerator for 30 minutes.

3 Roll the pastry out on a lightly floured surface and use to line the flan tin. Prick the pastry base and sides with a fork and line with nonstick baking parchment and baking beans. Bake blind in the preheated oven for 12 minutes. Remove the beans and baking parchment and continue to bake blind for 5 minutes.

4 Beat together the curd cheese and granulated sugar, then beat in the melted chocolate, saffron liquid, the milk and eggs, mix until blended thoroughly. Pour the mixture into the cooked flan case and place on a baking sheet.

5 Reduce the oven temperature to 190°C/375°F/Gas Mark 5 and bake for 15 minutes, then reduce the oven temperature to 180°C/350°F/Gas Mark 4 and continue to bake for 20–30 minutes or until set.

6 Remove the cheesecake from the oven and leave for 10 minutes before removing from the flan tin, if serving warm. If serving cold, leave in the flan tin to cool before removing and placing on a serving platter. Sprinkle with icing sugar before serving.

2

4

1

Orange Chocolate Cheesecake

INGREDIENTS

Serves 8

225 g/8 oz plain chocolate coated
   digestive biscuits
50 g/2 oz butter
450 g/1 lb mixed fruits, such as
   blueberries and raspberries
1 tbsp icing sugar, sifted
few sprigs of fresh mint, to decorate

For the filling:

450 g/1 lb soft cream cheese
1 tbsp gelatine
350 g/12 oz orange chocolate, broken
   into segments
600 ml/1 pint double cream

HELPFUL HINT

Alway add gelatine to the mixture
you are working with and whisk
well to evenly distribute it. Never
add the mixture to the gelatine or
it will tend to set in a lump.

1 Lightly oil and line a 20.5 cm/8 inch round loose-based cake tin with nonstick baking parchment. Place the biscuits in a polythene bag and crush using a rolling pin. Alternatively, use a food processor. Melt the butter in a medium-sized heavy-based saucepan, add the crushed biscuits and mix well. Press the biscuit mixture into the base of the lined tin, then chill in the refrigerator for 20 minutes.

2 For the filling, remove the cream cheese from the refrigerator at least 20 minutes before using, to allow the cheese to come to room temperature. Place the cream cheese in a bowl and beat until smooth, reserve.

3 Pour 4 tablespoons of water into a small bowl and sprinkle over the gelatine. Leave to stand for 5 minutes until spongy. Place the bowl over a saucepan of simmering water and allow to dissolve, stirring occasionally. Leave to cool slightly.

4 Melt the orange chocolate in a heatproof bowl set over a saucepan of simmering water, then leave to cool slightly.

5 Whip the cream until soft peaks form. Beat the gelatine and chocolate into cream cheese. Fold in the cream. Spoon into the tin and level the surface. Chill in the refrigerator for 4 hours until set.

6 Remove the cheesecake from the tin and place on a serving plate. Top with the fruits, dust with icing sugar and decorate with sprigs of mint.

1

5

6

Triple Chocolate Cheesecake

INGREDIENTS

Serves 6

For the base:

150 g/5 oz digestive biscuits, crushed
50 g/2 oz butter, melted

For the cheesecake:

75 g/3 oz white chocolate,
  roughly chopped
300 ml/½ pint double cream
50 g/2 oz caster sugar
3 medium eggs, beaten
400 g/14 oz full fat soft cream cheese
2 tbsp cornflour
75 g/3 oz plain dark chocolate,
  roughly chopped
75 g/3 oz milk chocolate,
  roughly chopped
fromage frais, to serve

HELPFUL HINT

Leaving the cheesecake to cool in the oven helps to prevent cracks from forming on the top. However, do not worry if the top does crack – it will not affect the flavour of the cheesecake.

1 Preheat the oven to 180°C/350°F/Gas Mark 4, 10 minutes before baking. Lightly oil a 23 x 7.5 cm/9 x 3 inch springform tin.

2 To make the base, mix together the crushed biscuits and melted butter. Press into the base of the tin and leave to set. Chill in the refrigerator.

3 Place the white chocolate and cream in a small heavy-based saucepan and heat gently until the chocolate has melted. Stir until smooth and reserve.

4 Beat the sugar and eggs together until light and creamy in colour, add the cream cheese and beat until the mixture is smooth and free from lumps.

5 Stir the reserved white chocolate cream together with the cornflour into the soft cream cheese mixture.

6 Add the dark and milk chocolate to the soft cream cheese mixture and mix lightly together until blended.

7 Spoon over the chilled base, place on a baking sheet and bake in the preheated oven for 1 hour.

8 Switch off the heat, open the oven door and leave the cheesecake to cool in the oven. Chill in the refrigerator for at least 6 hours before removing the cheesecake from the tin. Cut into slices and transfer to serving plates. Serve with fromage frais.

2

4

6

Baked Lemon & Sultana Cheesecake

INGREDIENTS

Cuts into 10 slices

275 g/10 oz caster sugar
50 g/2 oz butter
50 g/2 oz self-raising flour
½ level tsp baking powder
5 large eggs
450 g/1 lb cream cheese
40 g/1½ oz plain flour
grated rind of 1 lemon
3 tbsp fresh lemon juice
150 ml/¼ pint crème fraîche
75 g/3 oz sultanas

To decorate:

1 tbsp icing sugar
fresh blackcurrants or blueberries
mint leaves

TASTY TIP

Vary the flavour by adding a little freshly grated nutmeg and ½ teaspoon of ground cinnamon to the base in step 2. Add a little of both spices to the icing sugar before sprinkling.

1 Preheat the oven to 170°C/325°F/Gas Mark 3. Oil a 20.5 cm/8 inch loose-bottomed round cake tin with non-stick baking paper.

2 Beat 50 g/2 oz of the sugar and the butter together until light and creamy, then stir in the self-raising flour, baking powder and 1 egg.

3 Mix lightly together until well blended. Spoon into the prepared tin and spread the mixture over the base. Separate the 4 remaining eggs and reserve.

4 Blend the cheese in a food processor until soft. Gradually add the eggs yolks and sugar and blend until smooth. Turn into a bowl and stir in the rest of the flour, lemon rind and juice.

5 Mix lightly before adding the crème fraîche and sultanas, stirring well.

6 Whisk the egg whites until stiff, fold into the cheese mixture and pour into the tin. Tap lightly on the surface to remove any air bubbles. Bake in the preheated oven for about 1 hour, or until golden and firm.

7 Cover lightly if browning too much. Switch the oven off and leave in the oven to cool for 2–3 hours.

8 Remove the cheesecake from the oven and when completely cold remove from the tin. Sprinkle with the icing sugar, decorate with the blackcurrants or blueberries and mint leaves and serve.

3

4

5

Apricot & Almond Layer Cake

INGREDIENTS

Cuts into 8–10 slices

150 g/5 oz unsalted butter, softened

125 g/4 oz caster sugar

5 medium eggs, separated

150 g/5 oz plain dark chocolate,
  melted and cooled

150 g/5 oz self-raising flour, sifted

50 g/2 oz ground almonds

75 g/3 oz icing sugar, sifted

300 g/11 oz apricot jam

1 tbsp amaretto liqueur

125 g/4 oz unsalted butter, melted

125 g/4 oz plain dark
  chocolate, melted

1 Preheat the oven to 180°C/350°F/Gas Mark 4, 10 minutes before baking. Lightly oil and line 2 x 23 cm/9 inch round cake tins. Cream the butter and sugar together until light and fluffy, then beat in the egg yolks, one at a time, beating well after each addition. Stir in the cooled chocolate with 1 tablespoon of cooled boiled water, then fold in the flour and ground almonds.

2 Whisk the egg whites until stiff, then gradually whisk in the icing sugar, beating well after each addition. Whisk until the egg whites are stiff and glossy, then fold the egg whites into the chocolate mixture in 2 batches.

3 Divide the mixture evenly between the prepared tins and bake in the preheated oven for 30–40 minutes or until firm. Leave for 5 minutes before turning out onto wire racks. Leave to cool completely.

4 Split the cakes in half. Gently heat the jam, pass through a sieve and stir in the amaretto liqueur. Place 1 cake layer onto a serving plate. Spread with a little of the jam, then sandwich with the next layer. Repeat with all the layers and use any remaining jam to brush over the entire cake. Leave until the jam sets.

5 Meanwhile, beat the butter and chocolate together until smooth, then cool at room temperature until thick enough to spread. Cover the top and sides of the cake with the chocolate icing and leave to set before slicing and serving.

HELPFUL HINT

Use a very good-quality apricot jam as it is a major flavour in the finished cake.

1

2

4

Black & White Torte

INGREDIENTS

Cuts into 8–10 slices

4 medium eggs

150 g/5 oz caster sugar

50 g/2 oz cornflour

50 g/2 oz plain flour

50 g/2 oz self-raising flour

900 ml/1½ pints double cream

150 g/5 oz plain dark
   chocolate, chopped

300 g/11 oz white chocolate, chopped

6 tbsp Grand Marnier, or other
   orange liqueur

cocoa powder for dusting

1 Preheat the oven to 180°C/350°F/Gas Mark 4, 10 minutes before baking. Lightly oil and line a 23 cm/9 inch round cake tin. Beat the eggs and sugar in a large bowl until thick and creamy. Sift together the cornflour, plain flour and self-raising flour 3 times, then lightly fold into the egg mixture.

2 Spoon the mixture into the prepared tin and bake in the preheated oven for 35–40 minutes or until firm. Turn the cake out onto a wire rack and leave to cool.

3 Place 300 ml/½ pint of the double cream in a saucepan and bring to the boil. Immediately remove from the heat and add the plain chocolate and a further tablespoon of the liqueur. Stir until smooth. Repeat using the remaining cream, white chocolate and liqueur. Chill in the refrigerator for 2 hours, then whisk each mixture until thick and creamy.

4 Place the dark chocolate mixture in a piping bag fitted with a plain nozzle and place half the white chocolate mixture in a separate piping bag fitted with a plain nozzle. Reserve the remaining white chocolate mixture.

5 Split the cold cake horizontally into 2 layers. Brush or drizzle the remaining liqueur over the cakes. Put 1 layer onto a serving plate. Pipe alternating rings of white and dark chocolate mixture to cover the first layer of cake. Use the reserved white chocolate mixture to cover the top and sides of the cake. Dust with cocoa powder, cut into slices and serve. Store in the refrigerator.

1

3

4

Mocha Truffle Cake

INGREDIENTS

Cuts into 8–10 slices

3 medium eggs

125 g/4 oz caster sugar

40 g/1½ oz cornflour

40 g/1½ oz self-raising flour

2 tbsp cocoa powder

2 tbsp milk

2 tbsp coffee liqueur

100 g/3½ oz white chocolate, melted
  and cooled

200 g/7 oz plain dark chocolate,
  melted and cooled

600 ml/1 pint double cream

200 g/7 oz milk chocolate

100 g/3½ oz unsalted butter

1 Preheat the oven to 180°C/350°F/Gas Mark 4, 10 minutes before cooking. Lightly oil and line a deep 23 cm/9 inch round cake tin. Beat the eggs and sugar in a bowl until thick and creamy.

2 Sift together the cornflour, self-raising flour and cocoa powder and fold lightly into the egg mixture. Spoon into the prepared tin and bake in the preheated oven for 30 minutes or until firm. Turn out onto a wire rack and leave until cold. Split the cold cake horizontally into 2 layers. Mix together the milk and coffee liqueur and brush onto the cake layers.

3 Stir the cooled white chocolate into one bowl and the cooled plain dark chocolate into another one. Whip the cream until soft peaks form, then divide between the 2 bowls and stir. Place 1 layer of cake in a 23 cm/9 inch springform tin. Spread with half the white chocolate cream. Top with the dark chocolate cream, then the remaining white chocolate cream, finally place the remaining cake layer on top. Chill in the refrigerator for 4 hours or overnight until set.

4 When ready to serve, melt the milk chocolate and butter in a heatproof bowl set over a saucepan of simmering water and stir until smooth. Remove from the heat and leave until thick enough to spread, then use to cover the top and sides of the cake. Leave to set at room temperature, then chill in the refrigerator. Cut the cake into slices and serve.

HELPFUL HINT

Unless you are going to make a lot of chocolate or coffee desserts, liqueurs are very expensive to buy. Look for supermarket own label brands or miniatures.

Double Marble Cake

INGREDIENTS

Cuts into 8–10 slices

75 g/3 oz white chocolate

75 g/3 oz plain dark chocolate

175 g/6 oz caster sugar

175 g/6 oz butter

4 medium eggs, separated

125 g/4 oz plain flour, sifted

75 g/3 oz ground almonds

For the topping:

50 g/2 oz white chocolate, chopped

75 g/3 oz plain dark
  chocolate, chopped

50 ml/2 fl oz double cream

100 g/3½ oz unsalted butter

HELPFUL HINT

Place a folded tea towel under the mixing bowl when creaming or mixing by hand. This stops the bowl slipping around and makes the whole operation quicker and easier.

1 Preheat the oven to 180°C/350°F/Gas Mark 4, 10 minutes before baking. Lightly oil and line the base of a 20.5 cm/8 inch cake tin. Break the white and dark chocolate into small pieces, then place in 2 separate bowls placed over 2 pans of simmering water, ensuring that the bowls are not touching the water. Heat the chocolate until melted and smooth.

2 In a large bowl cream the sugar and butter together until light and fluffy. Beat in the egg yolks, 1 at a time and add a spoonful of flour after each addition. Stir in the ground almonds. In another bowl whisk the egg whites until stiff. Gently fold the egg whites and the remaining sifted flour alternately into the almond mixture until all the flour and egg whites have been incorporated. Divide the mixture between 2 bowls. Gently stir the white chocolate into 1 bowl, then add the dark chocolate to the other bowl.

3 Place alternating spoonfuls of the chocolate mixtures in the prepared cake tin. Using a skewer, swirl the mixtures together to get a marbled effect, then tap the tin on the work surface to level the mixture. Bake in the preheated oven for 40 minutes, or until cooked through, then leave to cool for 5 minutes in the tin, before turning out onto a wire rack to cool completely.

4 Melt the chocolate with the cream and butter and stir until smooth. Cool, then whisk until thick and swirl over the top of the cake.

2

3

4

Chocolate Buttermilk Cake

INGREDIENTS

Cuts into 8–10 slices

175 g/6 oz butter

1 tsp vanilla essence

350 g/12 oz caster sugar

4 medium eggs, separated

100 g/3½ oz self-raising flour

40 g/1½ oz cocoa powder

175 ml/6 fl oz buttermilk

200 g/7 oz plain dark chocolate

100 g/3½ oz butter

300 ml/½ pint double cream

1 Preheat the oven to 180°C/350°F/Gas Mark 4, 10 minutes before baking. Lightly oil and line a deep 23 cm/9 inch round cake tin. Cream together the butter, vanilla essence and sugar until light and fluffy, then beat in the egg yolks, 1 at a time.

2 Sift together the flour and cocoa powder and fold into the egg mixture together with the buttermilk. Whisk the egg whites until soft peaks form and fold carefully into the chocolate mixture in 2 batches. Spoon the mixture into the prepared tin and bake in the preheated oven for 1 hour or until firm. Cool slightly, then turn out onto a wire rack and leave until completely cold.

3 Place the chocolate and butter together in a heatproof bowl set over a saucepan of simmering water and heat until melted. Stir until smooth, then leave at room temperature until the chocolate is thick enough to spread.

4 Split the cake horizontally in half. Use some of the chocolate mixture to sandwich the 2 halves together. Spread and decorate the top of the cake with the remaining chocolate mixture. Finally, whip the cream until soft peaks form and use to spread around the sides of the cake. Chill in the refrigerator until required. Serve cut into slices. Store in the refrigerator.

TASTY TIP

If buttermilk is unavailable, measure 175 ml/6 fl oz of full fat milk and add 2 teaspoons of lemon juice or white wine vinegar. Leave to stand for 1 hour at room temperature and then use as above.

1

2

4

Peach & White Chocolate Gateau

INGREDIENTS

Cuts into 8–10 slices

175 g/6 oz unsalted butter, softened

2 tsp grated orange rind

175 g/6 oz caster sugar

3 medium eggs

100 g/3½ oz white chocolate, melted
  and cooled

225 g/8 oz self-raising flour, sifted

300 ml/½ pint double cream

40 g/1½ oz icing sugar

125 g/4 oz hazelnuts, toasted
  and chopped

For the peach filling:

2 ripe peaches, peeled and chopped

2 tbsp peach or orange liqueur

300 ml/½ pint double cream

40 g/1½ oz icing sugar

1. Preheat the oven to 170°C/325°F/Gas Mark 3, 10 minutes before baking. Lightly oil and line a deep 23 cm/9 inch round cake tin. Cream the butter, orange rind and sugar together until light and fluffy. Add the eggs, 1 at a time, beating well after each addition, then beat in the cooled white chocolate.

2. Add the flour and 175 ml/6 fl oz of water in 2 batches. Spoon into the prepared tin and bake in the preheated oven for 1½ hours or until firm. Leave to stand for at least 5 minutes before turning out onto a wire rack to cool completely.

3. To make the filling, place the peaches in a bowl and pour over the liqueur. Leave to stand for 30 minutes. Whip the cream with the icing sugar until soft peaks form, then fold in the peach mixture.

4. Split the cold cake in to 3 layers, place 1 layer on a serving plate and spread with half the peach filling. Top with a second sponge layer and spread with the remaining peach filling. Top with the remaining cake.

5. Whip the cream and icing sugar together until soft peaks form. Spread over the top and sides of the cake, piping some onto the top if liked. Press the hazelnuts into the side of cake and if liked sprinkle a few on top. Chill in the refrigerator until required. Serve cut into slices. Store the cake in the refrigerator.

TASTY TIP

When fresh peaches are out of season, use drained and chopped canned peaches instead.

Dark Chocolate Layered Torte

INGREDIENTS

Cuts into 10–12 slices

175 g/6 oz butter

1 tbsp instant coffee granules

150 g/ 5 oz plain dark chocolate

350 g/12 oz caster sugar

150 g/5 oz self-raising flour

125 g/4 oz plain flour

2 tbsp cocoa powder

2 medium eggs

1 tsp vanilla essence

215 g/7½ oz plain dark
   chocolate, melted

125 g/4 oz butter, melted

40 g/1½ oz icing sugar, sifted

2 tsp raspberry jam

2½ tbsp chocolate liqueur

100 g/3½ oz toasted flaked almonds

TASTY TIP

Use dark chocolate which has 70 per cent cocoa solids in this cake for the best flavour.

1. Preheat the oven to 150°C/300°F/Gas Mark 2, 10 minutes before baking. Lightly oil and line a 23 cm/9 inch square cake tin. Melt the butter in a saucepan, remove from the heat and stir in the coffee granules and 225 ml/8 fl oz hot water. Add the plain dark chocolate and sugar and stir until smooth, then pour into a bowl.

2. In another bowl, sift together the flours and cocoa powder. Using an electric whisk, whisk the sifted mixture into the chocolate mixture until smooth. Beat in the eggs and vanilla essence. Pour into the tin and bake in the preheated oven for 1¼ hours or until firm. Leave for at least 5 minutes before turning out onto a wire rack to cool.

3. Meanwhile, mix together 200 g/7 oz of the melted dark chocolate with the butter and icing sugar and beat until smooth. Leave to cool, then beat again. Reserve 4–5 tablespoons of the chocolate filling.

4. Cut the cooled cake in half to make 2 rectangles, then split each rectangle in 3 horizontally. Place 1 cake layer on a serving plate and spread thinly with the jam, then a thin layer of dark chocolate filling. Top with a second cake layer and sprinkle with a little liqueur, then spread thinly with filling. Repeat with the remaining cake layers, liqueur and filling.

5. Chill in the refrigerator for 2–3 hours or until firm. Cover the cake with the reserved chocolate filling and press the flaked almonds into the sides of the cake.

6. Place the remaining melted chocolate in a nonstick baking parchment piping bag. Snip a small hole in the tip and pipe thin lines 2 cm/¾ inch apart crossways over the cake. Drag a cocktail stick lengthways through the icing in alternating directions to create a feathered effect on the top. Serve.

3

4

6

Chocolate Mousse Sponge

INGREDIENTS

Cuts into 8–10 slices

3 medium eggs
75 g/3 oz caster sugar
1 tsp vanilla essence
50 g/2 oz self-raising flour, sifted
25 g/1 oz ground almonds
50 g/2 oz plain dark chocolate, grated
icing sugar, for dusting
freshly sliced strawberries,
  to decorate

For the mousse:

2 sheets gelatine
50 ml/2 fl oz double cream
100 g/3½ oz plain dark
  chocolate, chopped
1 tsp vanilla essence
4 medium egg whites
125 g/4 oz caster sugar

TASTY TIP

Sheet gelatine is very easy to use. Soak the gelatine as described in step 2, then squeeze out the excess liquid. It must be added to hot liquid, where it will melt on contact.

1 Preheat the oven to 180°C/350°F/Gas Mark 4, 10 minutes before baking. Lightly oil and line a 23 cm/9 inch round cake tin and lightly oil the sides of a 23 cm/9 inch springform tin. Whisk the eggs, sugar and vanilla essence until thick and creamy. Fold in the flour, ground almonds and dark chocolate. Spoon the mixture into the prepared round cake tin and bake in the preheated oven for 25 minutes or until firm. Turn out onto a wire rack to cool.

2 For the mousse, soak the gelatine in 50 ml/2 fl oz of cold water for 5 minutes until softened. Meanwhile, heat the double cream in a small saucepan, when almost boiling, remove from the heat and stir in the chocolate and vanilla essence. Stir until the chocolate melts. Squeeze the excess water out of the gelatine and add to the chocolate mixture. Stir until dissolved, then pour into a large bowl.

3 Whisk the egg whites until stiff, then gradually add the caster sugar, whisking well between each addition. Fold the egg white mixture into the chocolate mixture in 2 batches.

4 Split the cake into 2 layers. Place 1 layer in the bottom of the springform tin. Pour in the chocolate mousse mixture, then top with the second layer of cake. Chill in the refrigerator for 4 hours or until the mousse has set. Loosen the sides and remove the cake from the tin. Dust with icing sugar and decorate the top with a few freshly sliced strawberries. Serve cut into slices.

Chocolate Chiffon Cake

INGREDIENTS

Cuts into 10–12 slices

50 g/2 oz cocoa powder

300 g/11 oz self-raising flour

550 g/1¼ lb caster sugar

7 medium eggs, separated

125 ml/4 fl oz vegetable oil

1 tsp vanilla essence

75 g/3 oz walnuts

200 g/7 oz plain dark
   chocolate, melted

Fot the icing:

175 g/6 oz butter

275 g/10 oz icing sugar, sifted

2 tbsp cocoa powder, sifted

2 tbsp brandy

HELPFUL HINT

Do not overmix the mixture in step 2 or the cake will be heavy instead of very light and spongy.

1 Preheat the oven to 170°C/325°F/Gas Mark 3, 10 minutes before serving. Lightly oil and line a 23 cm/9 inch round cake tin. Lightly oil a baking sheet. Blend the cocoa powder with 175 ml/6 fl oz boiling water and leave to cool. Place the flour and 350 g/12 oz of the caster sugar in a large bowl, and add the cocoa mixture, egg yolks, oil and vanilla essence. Whisk until smooth and lighter in colour.

2 Whisk the egg whites in a clean, grease-free bowl until soft peaks form, then fold into the cocoa mixture.

3 Pour into the prepared tin and bake in the preheated oven for 1 hour or until firm. Leave for 5 minutes before turning out onto a wire rack to cool.

4 To make the icing, cream together 125 g/4 oz of the butter with the icing sugar, cocoa powder and brandy until smooth, then reserve. Melt the remaining butter and blend with 150 g/5 oz of the melted dark chocolate. Stir until smooth and then leave until thickened.

5 Place the remaining caster sugar into a heavy-based saucepan over a low heat and heat until the sugar has melted and is a deep golden brown.

6 Add the walnuts and the remaining melted chocolate to the melted sugar and pour onto the prepared baking sheet. Leave until cold and brittle, then chop finely. Reserve.

7 Split the cake into 3 layers, place 1 layer onto a serving plate and spread with half of the brandy butter icing. Top with a second cake layer and spread with the remaining brandy butter icing, arrange the third cake layer on top. Cover the cake with the thickened chocolate glaze. Sprinkle with the walnut praline and serve.

2

6

7

White Chocolate & Passion Fruit Cake

INGREDIENTS

Cuts into 8–10 slices

125 g/4 oz white chocolate

125 g/4 oz butter

225 g/8 oz caster sugar

2 medium eggs

125 ml/4 fl oz soured cream

200 g/7 oz plain flour, sifted

75 g/3 oz self-raising flour, sifted

125 g/4 oz white chocolate, coarsely
  grated, to decorate

For the icing:

200 g/7 oz caster sugar

4 tbsp passion fruit juice (about 8–10
  passion fruit, sieved)

1½ tbsp passion fruit seeds

250 g/9 oz unsalted butter

FOOD FACT

Passion fruit is available from large supermarkets. It adds a wonderful sweet/sour flavour that goes particularly well with white chocolate.

1 Preheat the oven to 180°C/350°F/Gas Mark 4, 10 minutes before baking. Lightly oil and line 2 x 20.5 cm/8 inch cake tins.

2 Melt the white chocolate in a heatproof bowl set over a saucepan of simmering water. Stir in 125 ml/4 fl oz warm water and stir, then leave to cool.

3 Whisk the butter and sugar together until light and fluffy, add the eggs, one at a time, beating well after each addition. Beat in the chocolate mixture, soured cream and sifted flours. Divide the mixture into 8 portions. Spread 1 portion into each of the tins. Bake in the preheated oven for 10 minutes, or until firm, then turn out onto wire racks. Repeat with the remaining mixture to make 8 cake layers.

4 To make the icing, place 125 ml/4 fl oz of water with 50 g/2 oz of the sugar in a saucepan. Heat gently, stirring, until the sugar has dissolved. Bring to the boil, simmer for 2 minutes. Remove from the heat and cool, then add 2 tablespoons of the passion fruit juice. Reserve.

5 Blend the remaining sugar with 50 ml/2 fl oz of water in a small saucepan and stir constantly over a low heat, without boiling, until the sugar has dissolved. Remove from the heat and cool. Stir in the remaining passion fruit juice and the seeds. Cool, then strain. Using an electric whisk, beat the butter in a bowl until very pale. Gradually beat in the syrup.

6 Place 1 layer of cake on a serving plate. Brush with the syrup and spread with a thin layer of icing. Repeat with the remaining cake, syrup and icing. Cover the cake with the remaining icing. Press the chocolate curls into the top and sides to decorate.

3

4

5

Sachertorte

INGREDIENTS

Cuts into 10–12 slices

150 g/5 oz plain dark chocolate

150 g/5 oz unsalted butter, softened

125 g/4 oz caster sugar, plus
  2 tbsp

3 medium eggs, separated

150 g/5 oz plain flour, sifted

To decorate:

225 g/8 oz apricot jam

125 g/4 oz plain dark
  chocolate, chopped

125 g/4 oz unsalted butter

25 g/1 oz milk chocolate

FOOD FACT

In 1832, the Viennese foreign minister asked a Vienna hotel to prepare an especially tempting cake. The head pastry chef was ill and so the task fell to second year apprentice, Franz Sacher, who presented this delightful cake.

1 Preheat the oven to 180°C/350°F/Gas Mark 4, 10 minutes before baking. Lightly oil and line a deep 23 cm/9 inch cake tin.

2 Melt the chocolate in a heatproof bowl set over a saucepan of simmering water. Stir in 1 tablespoon of water and leave to cool.

3 Beat the butter and 125 g/4 oz of the sugar together until light and fluffy. Beat in the egg yolks, one at a time, beating well between each addition. Stir in the melted chocolate, then the flour.

4 In a clean grease-free bowl, whisk the egg whites until stiff peaks form, then whisk in the remaining sugar. Fold into the chocolate mixture and spoon into the prepared tin. Bake in the pre-heated oven for 30 minutes until firm. Leave for 5 minutes, then turn out onto a wire rack to cool. Leave the cake upside down.

5 To decorate the cake, split the cold cake in 2 and place one half on a serving plate. Heat the jam and rub through a fine sieve.

6 Brush half the jam onto the first cake half, then cover with the remaining cake layer and brush with the remaining jam. Leave at room temperature for 1 hour or until the jam has set.

7 Place the plain dark chocolate with the butter into a heatproof bowl set over a saucepan of simmering water and heat until the chocolate melted. Stir occasionally until smooth, then leave until thickened. Use to cover the cake.

8 Melt the milk chocolate in a heatproof bowl set over a saucepan of simmering water. Place in a small greaseproof piping bag and snip a small hole at the tip. Pipe Sacher with a large 'S' on the top. Leave to set at room temperature.

3   4   5

Chocolate Roulade

INGREDIENTS

Cuts into 8 slices

200 g/7 oz plain dark chocolate
200 g/7 oz caster sugar
7 medium eggs, separated
300 ml/½ pint double cream
3 tbsp Cointreau or Grand Marnier
4 tbsp icing sugar for dusting

To decorate:
fresh raspberries
sprigs of fresh mint

1 Preheat the oven to 180°C/350°F/Gas Mark 4, 10 minutes before baking. Lightly oil and line a 33 cm x 23 cm/13 inch x 9 inch Swiss roll tin with nonstick baking parchment.

2 Break the chocolate into small pieces into a heatproof bowl set over a saucepan of simmering water. Leave until almost melted, stirring occasionally. Remove from the heat and leave to stand for 5 minutes.

3 Whisk the egg yolks with the sugar until pale and creamy and the whisk leaves a trail in the mixture when lifted, then carefully fold in the melted chocolate.

4 In a clean grease-free bowl, whisk the egg whites until stiff, then fold 1 large spoonful into the chocolate mixture.

5 Mix lightly, then gently fold in the remaining egg whites. Pour the mixture into the prepared tin and level the surface. Bake in the preheated oven for 20–25 minutes or until firm.

6 Remove the cake from the oven, leave in the tin and cover with a wire rack and a damp tea towel. Leave for 8 hours or overnight.

7 Dust a large sheet of nonstick baking parchment generously with 2 tablespoons of the icing sugar. Unwrap the cake and turn out onto the greaseproof paper. Remove the baking parchment.

8 Whip the cream with the liqueur until soft peaks form. Spread over the cake, leaving a 2.5 cm/1 inch border all round.

9 Using the paper to help, roll the cake up from a short end. Transfer to a serving plate, seam-side down, and dust with the remaining icing sugar. Decorate with fresh raspberries and mint. Serve.

TASTY TIP
Leaving the cake in the tin overnight gives it a fudgy texture and also means that the cake is less likely to break when it is rolled up.

1

6

9

Supreme Chocolate Gateau

INGREDIENTS

Cuts into 10–12 slices

For the cake:

175 g/6 oz self-raising flour, sifted

1½ tsp baking powder, sifted

3 tbsp cocoa powder, sifted

175 g/6 oz margarine or
  butter, softened

175 g/6 oz caster sugar

3 large eggs

To decorate:

350 g/12 oz plain dark chocolate

1 gelatine leaf

200 ml/7 fl oz double cream

75 g/3 oz butter

cocoa powder for dusting

HELPFUL HINT

If you prefer, make ordinary chocolate curls to decorate this cake.

1 Preheat the oven to 180°C/350°F/Gas Mark 4, 10 minutes before baking. Lightly oil and line 3 x 20.5 cm/8 inch round cake tins. Place all the cake ingredients into a bowl and whisk together until thick, add a little warm water if very thick. Divide the mixture evenly between the prepared tins. Bake in the preheated oven for 35–40 minutes until a skewer inserted in the centre comes out clean. Cool on wire racks.

2 Very gently heat 2 tablespoons of hot water with 50 g/2 oz of chocolate and stir until combined. Remove from the heat and leave for 5 minutes. Place the gelatine into a shallow dish and add 2 tablespoons of cold water. Leave for 5 minutes then squeeze out any excess water and add to the chocolate and water mixture. Stir until dissolved. Whip the double cream until just thickened. Add the chocolate mixture and continue whisking until soft peaks form. Leave until starting to set.

3 Place 1 of the cakes onto a serving plate and spread with half the cream mixture. Top with a second cake and the remaining cream, cover with the third cake and chill in the refrigerator until the cream has set.

4 Melt 175 g/6 oz of the chocolate with the butter and stir until smooth, leave until thickened. Melt the remaining chocolate. Cut 12 x 10 cm/4 inch squares of tinfoil. Spread the chocolate evenly over the squares to within 2.5 cm/1 inch of the edges. Refrigerate for 3–4 minutes until just set but not brittle. Gather up the corners and crimp together. Return to the refrigerator until firm.

5 Spread the chocolate and butter mixture over the top and sides of the cake. Remove the foil from the giant curls and use to decorate the top of the cake. Dust with cocoa powder and serve cut into wedges.

1

2

4

Chocolate Hazelnut Meringue Gateau

INGREDIENTS

Cuts into 8–10 slices

5 medium egg whites

275 g/10 oz caster sugar

125 g/4 oz hazelnuts, toasted and
  finely chopped

175 g/6 oz plain dark chocolate

100 g/3½ oz butter

3 medium eggs, separated, plus 1
  medium egg white

25 g/1 oz icing sugar

125 ml/4 fl oz double cream

hazelnuts, toasted and chopped,
  to decorate

TASTY TIP

This cake can be round. Make the
meringues into circles measuring
20.5 cm/8 inches. Trim to 18 cm/
7 inches before assembling.

1 Preheat the oven to 150°C/300°F/Gas Mark 2, 5 minutes before
baking. Cut 3 pieces of nonstick baking parchment into 30.5 cm x
12.5 cm/12 inch x 5 inch rectangles and then place onto 2 or 3
baking sheets.

2 Whisk the egg whites until stiff, add half the sugar and whisk until
the mixture is stiff, smooth and glossy. Whisk in the remaining sugar,
1 tablespoon at a time, beating well between each addition. When all
the sugar has been added whisk for 1 minute. Stir in the hazelnuts.

3 Spoon the meringue inside the marked rectangles spreading in
a continuous backwards and forwards movement. Bake in the
preheated oven for 1¼ hours, remove and leave until cold. Trim the
meringues until they measure 25.5 cm x 10 cm/10 inch x 4 inch.
Reserve all the trimmings.

4 Melt the chocolate and the butter in a heatproof bowl set over a
saucepan of gently simmering water and stir until smooth. Remove
from the heat and beat in the egg yolks. Whisk the egg whites until
stiff, then whisk in the icing sugar a little at a time. Fold the egg
whites into the chocolate mixture and chill in the refrigerator for
20–30 minutes, until thick enough to spread. Whip the double
cream until soft peaks form. Reserve.

5 Place 1 of the meringue layers onto a serving plate. Spread with
about half of the mousse mixture, then top with a second meringue
layer. Spread the remaining mouse mixture over the top with the
third meringue. Spread the cream over the top and sprinkle with the
chopped hazelnuts. Chill in the refrigerator for at least 4 hours and
up to 24 hours. Serve cut into slices.

3

4

5

Black Forest Gateau

INGREDIENTS

Cuts 10–12 slices

250 g/9 oz butter

1 tbsp instant coffee granules

350 ml/12 fl oz hot water

200 g/7 oz plain dark chocolate, chopped or broken

400 g/14 oz caster sugar

225 g/8 oz self-raising flour

150 g/5 oz plain flour

50 g/2 oz cocoa powder

2 medium eggs

2 tsp vanilla essence

2 x 400 g cans stoned cherries in juice

2 tsp arrowroot

600 ml/1 pint double cream

50 ml/2 fl oz kirsch

HELPFUL HINT

The cake can be assembled and served straightaway but will benefit from being refrigerated for 1–2 hours so that the cream sets slightly. This will make slicing easier.

1 Preheat the oven to 150°C/300°F/Gas Mark 2, 5 minutes before serving. Lightly oil and line a deep 23 cm/9 inch cake tin.

2 Melt the butter in a large saucepan. Blend the coffee with the hot water, add to the butter with the chocolate and sugar and heat gently, stirring until smooth. Pour into a large bowl and leave until just warm.

3 Sift together the flours and cocoa powder. Using an electric mixer, whisk the warm chocolate mixture on a low speed, then gradually whisk in the dry ingredients. Whisk in the eggs 1 at a time, then the vanilla essence.

4 Pour the mixture into the prepared tin and bake in the preheated oven for 1 hour 45 minutes or until firm and a skewer inserted into the centre comes out clean. Leave in the tin for 5 minutes to cool slightly before turning out onto a wire rack.

5 Place the cherries and their juice in a small saucepan and heat gently. Blend the arrowroot with 2 teaspoons of water until smooth, then stir into the cherries. Cook, stirring, until the liquid thickens. Simmer very gently for 2 minutes, then leave until cold.

6 Whisk the double cream until thick. Trim the top of the cake if necessary, then split the cake into 3 layers.

7 Brush the base of the cake with half the kirsch. Top with a layer of cream and one-third of the cherries. Repeat the layering, then place the third layer on top. Reserve a little cream for decorating and use the remainder to cover the top and sides of the cake. Pipe a decorative edge around the cake, then arrange the remaining cherries in the centre and serve.

3

5

6

Whole Orange & Chocolate Cake with Marmalade Cream

INGREDIENTS

Cuts into 6–8 slices

1 small orange, scrubbed
2 medium eggs, separated, plus
  1 whole egg
150 g/5 oz caster sugar
125 g/4 oz ground almonds
75 g/3 oz plain dark chocolate, melted
100 ml/3½ fl oz double cream
200 g/7 oz full fat soft cheese
25 g/1 oz icing sugar
2 tbsp orange marmalade
orange zest, to decorate

TASTY TIP

This cake contains no flour and is therefore likely to sink in the centre on cooling. This is normal and does not mean that the cake is not cooked.

1 Preheat the oven to 180°C/350°F/Gas Mark 4, 10 minutes before baking. Lightly oil and line the base of a 900 g/2 lb loaf tin. Place the orange in a small saucepan, cover with cold water and bring to the boil. Simmer for 1 hour until completely soft. Drain and leave to cool.

2 Place 2 egg yolks, 1 whole egg and the sugar in a heatproof bowl set over a pan of simmering water and whisk until doubled in bulk. Remove from the heat and continue to whisk for 5 minutes until cooled.

3 Cut the whole orange in half and discard the seeds, then place into a food processor or blender and blend to a purée. Carefully fold the purée into the egg yolk mixture with the ground almonds and melted chocolate.

4 Whisk the egg whites until stiff peaks form. Fold a large spoonful of the egg whites into the chocolate mixture, then gently fold the remaining egg whites into the mixture.

5 Pour into the prepared tin and bake in the preheated oven for 50 minutes, or until firm and a skewer inserted into the centre comes out clean. Cool in the tin before turning out of the tin and carefully discarding the lining paper.

6 Meanwhile, whip the double cream until just thickened. In another bowl, blend the soft cheese with the icing sugar and marmalade until smooth, then fold in the double cream.

7 Chill the marmalade cream in the refrigerator until required. Decorate with orange zest and serve the cake cut in slices with the marmalade cream.

2

3

6

Grated Chocolate Roulade

INGREDIENTS

Cuts into 8 slices

4 medium eggs, separated

125 g/4 oz caster sugar

60 g/2½ oz plain dark
    chocolate, grated

75 g/3 oz self-raising flour, sifted

2 tbsp caster sugar, plus extra
    for sprinkling

150 ml/¼ pint double cream

2 tsp icing sugar

1 tsp vanilla essence

chocolate curls, to decorate

1 Preheat the oven to 180°C/350°F/Gas Mark 4, 10 minutes before serving. Lightly oil and line a 20.5 cm x 30.5 cm/8 inch x 12 inch Swiss roll tin. Beat the egg yolks and sugar with an electric mixer for 5 minutes or until thick, then stir in 2 tablespoons of hot water and the grated chocolate. Finally fold in the sifted flour.

2 Whisk the egg whites until stiff, then fold 1–2 tablespoons of egg white into the chocolate mixture. Mix lightly, then gently fold in the remaining egg white. Pour into the prepared tin and bake in the preheated oven for about 12 minutes or until firm.

3 Place a large sheet of nonstick baking parchment onto a work surface and sprinkle liberally with caster sugar. Turn the cake onto the baking parchment, discard the lining paper and trim away the crisp edges. Roll up as for a Swiss roll cake, leave for 2 minutes, then unroll and leave to cool.

4 Beat the double cream with the icing sugar and vanilla essence until thick. Reserve a little for decoration, then spread the remaining cream over the cake, leaving a 2.5 cm/1 inch border all round. Using the greaseproof paper, roll up from a short end.

5 Carefully transfer the roulade to a large serving plate and use the reserved cream to decorate the top. Add the chocolate curls just before serving, then cut into slices and serve. Store in the refrigerator.

HELPFUL HINT

Make sure to leave a border around the cream before rolling up the roulade or all the cream with squeeze out of the ends.

2

3

4

White Chocolate & Raspberry Mousse Gateau

INGREDIENTS

Cuts into 8 slices

4 medium eggs

125 g/4 oz caster sugar

75 g/3 oz plain flour, sifted

25 g/1 oz cornflour, sifted

3 gelatine leaves

450 g/1 lb raspberries, thawed
  if frozen

400 g/14 oz white chocolate

200 g/7 oz plain fromage frais

2 medium egg whites

25 g/1 oz caster sugar

4 tbsp raspberry or orange liqueur

200 ml/7 fl oz double cream

fresh raspberries, halved, to decorate

HELPFUL HINT

Do not try to wrap the chocolate-covered parchment around the cake before it is nearly set or it will run down and be uneven.

1. Preheat the oven to 190°C/375°F/Gas Mark 5, 10 minutes before baking. Oil and line 2 x 23 cm/9 inch cake tins. Whisk the eggs and sugar until thick and creamy and the whisk leaves a trail in the mixture. Fold in the flour and cornflour, then divide between the tins. Bake in the preheated oven for 12–15 minutes or until risen and firm. Cool in the tins, then turn out onto wire racks.

2. Place the gelatine with 4 tablespoons of cold water in a dish and leave to soften for 5 minutes. Purée half the raspberries, press through a sieve, then heat until nearly boiling. Squeeze out excess water from the gelatine, add to the purée and stir until dissolved. Reserve.

3. Melt 175 g/6 oz of the chocolate in a bowl set over a saucepan of simmering water. Leave to cool, then stir in the fromage frais and purée. Whisk the egg whites until stiff and whisk in the sugar. Fold into the raspberry mixture with the rest of the raspberries.

4. Line the sides of a 23 cm/9 inch springform tin with nonstick baking parchment. Place 1 layer of sponge in the base and sprinkle with half the liqueur. Pour in the raspberry mixture and top with the second sponge. Brush with the remaining liqueur. Press down and chill in the refrigerator for 4 hours. Unmould onto a plate.

5. Cut a strip of double thickness nonstick baking parchment to fit around the cake and stand 1 cm/½ inch higher. Melt the remaining white chocolate and spread thickly onto the parchment. Leave until just setting. Wrap around the cake and freeze for 15 minutes. Peel away the parchment. Whip the cream until thick and spread over the top. Decorate with raspberries.

1

2

4

Chocolate Orange Fudge Cake

INGREDIENTS

Cuts into 8–10 slices

60 g/2½ oz cocoa powder

grated zest of 1 orange

350 g/12 oz self-raising flour

2 tsp baking powder

1 tsp bicarbonate of soda

½ tsp salt

225 g/8 oz light soft brown sugar

175 g/6 oz butter, softened

3 medium eggs

1 tsp vanilla essence

250 ml/9 fl oz soured cream

6 tbsp butter

6 tbsp milk

thinly pared rind of 1 orange

6 tbsp cocoa powder

250 g/9 oz icing sugar, sifted

1 Preheat the oven to 180°C/350°F/Gas Mark 4, 10 minutes before baking. Lightly oil and line 2 x 23 cm/9 inch round cake tins with nonstick baking parchment. Blend the cocoa powder and 50 ml/ 2 fl oz of boiling water until smooth. Stir in the orange zest and reserve. Sift together the flour, baking powder, bicarbonate of soda and salt, then reserve. Cream together the sugar and softened butter and beat in the eggs, 1 at a time, then the cocoa mixture and vanilla essence. Finally, stir in the flour mixture and the soured cream in alternate spoonfuls.

2 Divide the mixture between the prepared tins and bake in the preheated oven for 35 minutes, or until the edges of the cake pull away from the tin and the tops spring back when lightly pressed. Cool in the tins for 10 minutes, then turn out onto wire racks until cold.

3 Gently heat together the butter and milk with the pared orange rind. Simmer for 10 minutes, stirring occasionally. Remove from the heat and discard the orange rind.

4 Pour the warm orange and milk mixture into a large bowl and stir in the cocoa powder. Gradually beat in the sifted icing sugar and beat until the icing is smooth and spreadable. Place 1 cake onto a large serving plate. Top with about one-quarter of the icing, place the second cake on top, then cover the cake completely with the remaining icing. Serve.

HELPFUL HINT

This cake keeps exceptionally well in an airtight container for up to 5 days.

Cranberry & White Chocolate Cake

INGREDIENTS

Serves 4

225 g/8 oz butter, softened

250 g/9 oz full fat soft cheese

150 g/5 oz light soft brown sugar

200 g/7 oz caster sugar

grated zest of ½ orange

1 tsp vanilla essence

4 medium eggs

375 g/13 oz plain flour

2 tsp baking powder

200 g/7 oz cranberries, thawed
   if frozen

225 g/8 oz white chocolate,
   coarsely chopped

2 tbsp orange juice

1 Preheat the oven to 180°C/350°F/Gas Mark 4, 10 minutes before baking. Lightly oil and flour a 23 cm/9 inch kugelhopf tin or ring tin. Using an electric mixer, cream the butter and cheese with the sugars until light and fluffy. Add the grated orange zest and vanilla essence and beat until smooth, then beat in the eggs, 1 at a time.

2 Sift the flour and baking powder together and stir into the creamed mixture, beating well after each addition. Fold in the cranberries and 175 g/6 oz of the white chocolate. Spoon into the prepared tin and bake in the preheated oven for 1 hour, or until firm and a skewer inserted into the centre comes out clean. Cool in the tin before turning out onto on a wire rack.

3 Melt the remaining white chocolate, stir until smooth, then stir in the orange juice and leave to cool until thickened. Transfer the cake to a serving plate and spoon over the white chocolate and orange glaze. Leave to set.

TASTY TIP

If fresh or frozen cranberries are not available substitute with either peeled and diced Bramley cooking apple, raisins, dried cranberries or ready-to-eat chopped dried apricots.

Fresh Strawberry Sponge Cake

INGREDIENTS

Serves 8–10

175 g/6 oz unsalted
  butter, softened
175 g/6 oz caster sugar
1 tsp vanilla essence
3 large eggs, beaten
175 g/6 oz self-raising flour
150 ml/¼ pint double cream
2 tbsp icing sugar, sifted
225 g/8 oz fresh strawberries, hulled
  and chopped
few extra strawberries, to decorate

HELPFUL HINT

For sponge cakes, it is important to achieve the correct consistency of the uncooked mixture. Check it after folding in the flour by tapping a spoonful of the mixture on the side of the bowl. If it drops easily, 'dropping' consistency has been reached. If it is too stiff, fold in a tablespoon of cooled boiled water.

1 Preheat the oven to 190°C/375°F/Gas Mark 5, 10 minutes before baking. Lightly oil and line the bases of 2 x 20.5 cm/8 inch round cake tins with greaseproof or baking paper.

2 Using an electric whisk, beat the butter, sugar and vanilla essence until pale and fluffy. Gradually beat in the eggs a little at a time, beating well between each addition.

3 Sift half the flour over the mixture and using a metal spoon or rubber spatula gently fold into the mixture. Sift over the remaining flour and fold in until just blended.

4 Divide the mixture between the tins, spreading evenly. Gently smooth the surfaces with the back of a spoon. Bake in the centre of the preheated oven for 20–25 minutes, or until well risen and golden.

5 Remove and leave to cool before turning out on to a wire rack. Whip the cream with 1 tablespoon of the icing sugar until it forms soft peaks. Fold in the chopped strawberries.

6 Spread 1 cake layer evenly with the mixture and top with the second cake layer, rounded side up.

7 Thickly dust the cake with icing sugar and decorate with the reserved strawberries. Carefully slide on to a serving plate and serve.

1

2

3

Almond Angel Cake with Amaretto Cream

INGREDIENTS

Cuts into 10–12 slices

175 g/6 oz icing sugar, plus
   2–3 tbsp
150 g/5 oz plain flour
350 ml/12 fl oz egg whites (about 10
   large egg whites)
1½ tsp cream of tartar
½ tsp vanilla essence
1 tsp almond essence
¼ tsp salt
200 g/7 oz caster sugar
175 ml/6 fl oz double cream
2 tablespoons Amaretto liqueur
fresh raspberries, to decorate

FOOD FACT

Angel cake has a very light and delicate texture, and can be difficult to slice. For best results, use 2 forks gently to separate a portion of the cake.

1   Preheat the oven to 180°C/350°F/Gas Mark 4, 10 minutes before baking. Sift together the 175 g/6 oz icing sugar and flour. Stir to blend, then sift again and reserve.

2   Using an electric whisk, beat the egg whites, cream of tartar, vanilla essence, ½ teaspoon of almond essence and salt on medium speed until soft peaks form. Gradually add the caster sugar, 2 tablespoons at a time, beating well after each addition, until stiff peaks form.

3   Sift about one-third of the flour mixture over the egg white mixture and using a metal spoon or rubber spatula, gently fold into the egg white mixture. Repeat, folding the flour mixture into the egg white mixture in 2 more batches. Spoon gently into an ungreased angel food cake tin or 25.5 cm/10 inch tube tin.

4   Bake in the preheated oven until risen and golden on top and the surface springs back quickly when gently pressed with a clean finger. Immediately invert the cake tin and cool completely in the tin.

5   When cool, carefully run a sharp knife around the edge of the tin and the centre ring to loosen the cake from the edge. Using the fingertips, ease the cake from the tin and invert on to a cake plate. Thickly dust the cake with the extra icing sugar.

6   Whip the cream with the remaining almond essence, Amaretto liqueur and a little more icing sugar, until soft peaks form.

7   Fill a piping bag fitted with a star nozzle with half the cream and pipe around the bottom edge of the cake. Decorate the edge with the fresh raspberries and serve the remaining cream separately.

1

3

7

Luxury Carrot Cake

INGREDIENTS

Cuts into 12 slices

275 g/10 oz plain flour

2 tsp baking powder

1 tsp bicarbonate of soda

1 tsp salt

2 tsp ground cinnamon

1 tsp ground ginger

200 g/7 oz dark soft brown sugar

100 g/3½ oz caster sugar

4 large eggs, beaten

250 ml/9 fl oz sunflower oil

1 tbsp vanilla essence

4 carrots, peeled and shredded
  (about 450 g/1 lb)

380 g/14 oz can crushed pineapple,
  well drained

125 g/4 oz pecans or walnuts, toasted
  and chopped

For the frosting:

175 g/6 oz cream cheese, softened

50 g/2 oz butter, softened

1 tsp vanilla essence

225 g/8 oz icing sugar, sifted

1–2 tbsp milk

1 Preheat the oven to 180°C/350°F/Gas Mark 4, 10 minutes before baking. Lightly oil a 33 x 23 cm/13 x 9 inch baking tin. Line the base with non-stick baking paper, oil and dust with flour.

2 Sift the first 6 ingredients into a large bowl and stir in the sugars to blend. Make a well in the centre.

3 Beat the eggs, oil and vanilla essence together and pour into the well. Using an electric whisk, gradually beat, drawing in the flour mixture from the side until a smooth batter forms. Stir in the carrots, crushed pineapple and chopped nuts until blended.

4 Pour into the prepared tin and smooth the surface evenly. Bake in the preheated oven for 50 minutes, or until firm and a skewer inserted into the centre comes out clean. Remove from the oven and leave to cool before removing from the tin and discarding the lining paper.

5 For the frosting, beat the cream cheese, butter and vanilla essence together until smooth, then gradually beat in the icing sugar until the frosting is smooth. Add a little milk, if necessary. Spread the frosting over the top. Refrigerate for about 1 hour to set the frosting, then cut into squares and serve.

2

3

5

White Chocolate Cheesecake

INGREDIENTS

Cuts into 16 slices

For the base:
150 g/5 oz digestive biscuits
50 g/2 oz whole almonds,
  lightly toasted
50 g/2 oz butter, melted
½ tsp almond essence

For the filling:
350 g/12 oz good-quality white
  chocolate, chopped
125 ml/4 fl oz double cream
700 g/1½ lb cream
  cheese, softened
50 g/2 oz caster sugar
4 large eggs
2 tbsp Amaretto or
  almond-flavour liqueur

For the topping:
450 ml/¾ pint soured cream
50 g/2 oz caster sugar
½ tsp almond or vanilla essence
white chocolate curls,
  to decorate

1. Preheat the oven to 180°C/350°F/Gas Mark 4, 10 minutes before baking. Lightly oil a 23 x 7.5 cm/9 x 3 inch springform tin. Crush the biscuits and almonds in a food processor to form fine crumbs. Pour in the butter and almond essence and blend. Pour the crumbs into the tin and using the back of a spoon, press on to the bottom and up the sides to within 1 cm/½ inch of the top of the tin edge.

2. Bake in the preheated oven for 5 minutes to set. Remove and transfer to a wire rack. Reduce the oven temperature to 150°C/300°F/Gas Mark 2.

3. Heat the white chocolate and cream in a saucepan over a low heat, stirring constantly until melted. Remove and cool.

4. Beat the cream cheese and sugar until smooth. Add the eggs, one at a time, beating well after each addition. Slowly beat in the cooled white chocolate cream and the Amaretto and pour into the baked crust. Place on a baking tray and bake for 45–55 minutes, until the edge of the cake is firm, but the centre is slightly soft. Reduce the oven temperature if the top begins to brown. Remove to a wire rack and increase the temperature to 200°C/400°F/Gas Mark 6.

5. To make the topping, beat the soured cream, sugar and almond or vanilla essence until smooth and gently pour over the cheesecake, tilting the pan to distribute the topping evenly. Alternatively spread with a metal palette knife.

6. Bake for another 5 minutes to set. Turn off the oven and leave the door halfway open for about 1 hour. Transfer to a wire rack and run a sharp knife around the edge of the crust to separate from the tin. Cool and refrigerate until chilled. Remove from the tin, decorate with white chocolate curls and serve.

1

4

5

Rich Devil's Food Cake

INGREDIENTS

Cuts into 12–16 slices

450 g/1 lb plain flour
1 tbsp bicarbonate of soda
½ tsp salt
75 g/3 oz cocoa powder
300 ml/½ pint milk
150 g/5 oz butter, softened
400 g/14 oz soft dark brown sugar
2 tsp vanilla essence
4 large eggs

For the chocolate fudge frosting:

275 g/10 oz caster sugar
½ tsp salt
125 g/4 oz plain dark
  chocolate, chopped
225 ml/8 fl oz milk
2 tbsp golden syrup
125 g/4 oz butter, diced
2 tsp vanilla essence

1 Preheat the oven to 180°C/350°F/Gas Mark 4, 10 minutes before baking. Lightly oil and line the bases of 3 x 23 cm/9 inch cake tins with greaseproof or baking paper. Sift the flour, bicarbonate of soda and salt into a bowl.

2 Sift the cocoa powder into another bowl and gradually whisk in a little of the milk to form a paste. Continue whisking in the milk until a smooth mixture results.

3 Beat the butter, sugar and vanilla essence until light and fluffy then gradually beat in the eggs, beating well after each addition. Stir in the flour and cocoa mixtures alternately in 3 or 4 batches.

4 Divide the mixture evenly among the 3 tins, smoothing the surfaces evenly. Bake in the preheated oven for 25–35 minutes, until cooked and firm to the touch. Remove, cool and turn out on to a wire rack. Discard the lining paper.

5 To make the frosting, put the sugar, salt and chocolate into a heavy based saucepan and stir in the milk until blended. Add the golden syrup and butter. Bring the mixture to the boil over a medium-high heat, stirring to help dissolve the sugar.

6 Boil for 1 minute, stirring constantly. Remove from the heat, stir in the vanilla essence and cool. When cool, whisk until thickened and slightly lightened in colour.

7 Sandwich the 3 cake layers together with about a third of the frosting, placing the third cake layer with the flat side up. Transfer the cake to a serving plate and, using a metal palette knife, spread the remaining frosting over the top and sides. Swirl the top to create a decorative effect and serve.

2

5

7

Italian Polenta Cake with Mascarpone Cream

INGREDIENTS

Cuts into 6–8 slices

1 tsp butter and flour for the tin

100 g/3½ oz plain flour

40 g/1½ oz polenta or
  yellow cornmeal

1 tsp baking powder

¼ tsp salt

grated zest of 1 lemon

2 large eggs

150 g/5 oz caster sugar

5 tbsp milk

½ tsp almond essence

2 tbsp raisins or sultanas

75 g/3 oz unsalted
  butter, softened

2 medium dessert pears, peeled,
  cored and thinly sliced

2 tbsp apricot jam

175 g/6 oz mascarpone cheese

1–2 tsp sugar

50 ml/2 fl oz double cream

2 tbsp Amaretto liqueur or rum

2–3 tbsp toasted flaked almonds

icing sugar, to dust

1 Preheat the oven to 190°C/375°F/Gas Mark 5, 10 minutes before baking. Butter a 23 cm/9 inch springform tin. Dust lightly with flour.

2 Stir the flour, polenta or cornmeal, baking powder, salt and lemon zest together. Beat the eggs and half the sugar until light and fluffy. Slowly beat in the milk and almond essence.

3 Stir in the raisins or sultanas, then beat in the flour mixture and 50 g/2 oz of the butter.

4 Spoon into the tin and smooth the top evenly. Arrange the pear slices on top in overlapping concentric circles.

5 Melt the remaining butter and brush over the pear slices. Sprinkle with the rest of the sugar.

6 Bake in the preheated oven for about 40 minutes, until puffed and golden and the edges of the pears are lightly caramelised. Transfer to a wire rack. Reserve to cool in the tin for 15 minutes.

7 Remove the cake from the tin. Heat the apricot jam with 1 tablespoon of water and brush over the top of the cake to glaze.

8 Beat the mascarpone cheese with the sugar to taste, the cream and Amaretto or rum until smooth and forming a soft dropping consistency. Serve with the polenta cake.

9 When cool, sprinkle the almonds over the polenta cake and dust generously with the icing sugar. Serve the cake with the liqueur-flavoured mascarpone cream on the side.

1

4

7

Autumn Bramley Apple Cake

INGREDIENTS

Cuts into 8–10 slices

225 g/8 oz self-raising flour

1½ tsp baking powder

150 g/5 oz margarine, softened

150 g/5 oz caster sugar, plus extra
   for sprinkling

1 tsp vanilla essence

2 large eggs, beaten

1.1 kg/2½2 lbs Bramley cooking
   apples, peeled, cored and sliced

1 tbsp lemon juice

½ tsp ground cinnamon

fresh custard sauce or cream,
   to serve

FOOD FACT

Cooking apples are extremely versatile, as they can be baked, puréed, poached and used in cakes and pies as well as savoury foods. Apples have a good soluble fibre content and are an important aid for slimmers as they keep hunger pangs at bay.

1 Preheat the oven to 170°C/325°F/Gas Mark 3, 10 minutes before baking. Lightly oil and line the base of a 20.5 cm/8 inch deep cake tin with non-stick baking or greaseproof paper. Sift the flour and baking powder into a small bowl.

2 Beat the margarine, sugar and vanilla essence until light and fluffy. Gradually beat in the eggs a little at a time, beating well after each addition. Stir in the flour.

3 Spoon about one-third of the mixture into the tin, smoothing the surface. Toss the apple slices in the lemon juice and cinnamon and spoon over the cake mixture, making a thick even layer. Spread the remaining mixture over the apple layer to the edge of the tin, making sure the apples are covered. Smooth the top with the back of a wet spoon and sprinkle generously with sugar.

4 Bake in the preheated oven for 1½ hours, or until well risen and golden, the apples are tender and the centre of the cake springs back when pressed lightly. (Reduce the oven temperature slightly and cover the cake loosely with tinfoil if the top browns too quickly.)

5 Transfer to a wire rack and cool for about 20 minutes in the tin. Run a thin knife blade between the cake and the the tin to loosen the cake and invert on to a paper-lined rack. Turn the cake the right way up and cool. Serve with the custard sauce or cream.

3

3

5

Christmas Cranberry Chocolate Roulade

INGREDIENTS

Cuts into 12–14 slices

For the chocolate ganache frosting:
300 ml/½ pint double cream
350 g/12 oz plain dark
   chocolate, chopped
2 tbsp brandy (optional)

For the roulade:
5 large eggs, separated
3 tbsp cocoa powder, sifted, plus
   extra for dusting
125 g/4 oz icing sugar, sifted, plus
   extra for dusting
¼ tsp cream of tartar

For the filling:
175 g/6 oz cranberry sauce
½ tbsp brandy (optional)
450 ml/¾ pint double cream,
   whipped to soft peaks

To decorate:
caramelised orange strips
dried cranberries

1 Preheat the oven to 200°C /400°F/Gas Mark 6. Bring the cream to the boil over a medium heat. Remove from the heat and add all of the chocolate, stirring until melted. Stir in the brandy, if using and strain into a medium bowl. Cool, then refrigerate for 6–8 hours.

2 Lightly oil and line a 39 x 26 cm/15 ½ x 10½ inch Swiss roll tin with non-stick baking paper. Using an electric whisk, beat the egg yolks until thick and creamy. Slowly beat in the cocoa powder and half the icing sugar and reserve. Whisk the egg whites and cream of tartar into soft peaks. Gradually whisk in the remaining sugar until the mixture is stiff and glossy. Gently fold the yolk mixture into the egg whites with a metal spoon or rubber spatula. Spread evenly into the tin.

3 Bake in the preheated oven for 15 minutes. Remove and invert on to a large sheet of greaseproof paper, dusted with cocoa powder. Cut off the crisp edges of the cake then roll up. Leave on a wire rack until cold.

4 For the filling, heat the cranberry sauce with the brandy, if using, until warm and spreadable. Unroll the cooled cake and spread with the cranberry sauce. Allow to cool and set. Carefully spoon the whipped cream over the surface and spread to within 2.5 cm/1 inch of the edges. Re-roll the cake. Transfer to a cake plate or tray.

5 Allow the chocolate ganache to soften at room temperature, then beat until soft and of a spreadable consistency. Spread over the roulade and, using a fork, mark the roulade with ridges to resemble tree bark. Dust with icing sugar. Decorate with the caramelised orange strips and dried cranberries and serve.

3

4

5

Buttery Passion Fruit Madeira Cake

INGREDIENTS

Cuts into 8–10 slices

210 g/7½ oz plain flour

1 tsp baking powder

175 g/6 oz unsalted
   butter, softened

250 g/9 oz caster sugar, plus 1 tsp

grated zest of 1 orange

1 tsp vanilla essence

3 medium eggs, beaten

2 tbsp milk

6 ripe passion fruits

50 g/2 oz icing sugar

icing sugar, to dust

FOOD FACT

Regardless of its name, Madeira cake does not actually originate from the Portuguese-owned island of Madeira. It is, in fact, a traditional English favourite which acquired its name because the cake was often served with the fortified wine, Madeira.

1   Preheat the oven to 180°C/350°F/Gas Mark 4, 10 minutes before baking. Lightly oil and line the base of a 23 x 12.5 cm/9 x 5 inch loaf tin with greaseproof paper. Sift the flour and baking powder into a bowl and reserve.

2   Beat the butter, sugar, orange zest and vanilla essence until light and fluffy, then gradually beat in the eggs, 1 tablespoon at a time, beating well after each addition. If the mixture appears to curdle or separate, beat in a little of the flour mixture.

3   Fold in the flour mixture with the milk until just blended. Do not over mix. Spoon lightly into the prepared tin and smooth the top evenly. Sprinkle lightly with the teaspoon of caster sugar.

4   Bake in the preheated oven for 55 minutes, or until well risen and golden brown. Remove from the oven and leave to cool for 15–20 minutes. Turn the cake out of the tin and discard the lining paper.

5   Cut the passion fruits in half and scoop out the pulp into a sieve set over a bowl. Press the juice through using a rubber spatula or wooden spoon. Stir in the icing sugar and stir to dissolve, adding a little extra sugar if necessary.

6   Using a skewer, pierce holes all over the cake. Slowly spoon the passion fruit glaze over the cake and allow to seep in. Gently invert the cake on to a wire rack, then turn it back the right way up. Dust with icing sugar and cool completely. Serve the Madeira cake cold.

3

5

6

French Chocolate Pecan Torte

INGREDIENTS

Cuts into 16 slices

200 g/7 oz plain dark
  chocolate, chopped
150 g/5 oz butter, diced
4 large eggs
100 g/3½ oz caster sugar
2 tsp vanilla essence
125 g/4 oz pecans, finely ground
2 tsp ground cinnamon
24 pecan halves, lightly toasted,
  to decorate

For the chocolate glaze:

125 g/4 oz plain dark
  chocolate, chopped
60 g/2½ oz butter, diced
2 tbsp clear honey
¼ tsp ground cinnamon

FOOD FACT

Although this recipe is French, the torte actually originates from Germany, and tends to be a very rich cake-like dessert. It is delicious served with a fruity mixed berry compote.

1   Preheat the oven to 180°C/350°F/Gas Mark 4, 10 minutes before baking. Lightly butter and line a 20.5 x 5 cm/8 x 2 inch springform tin with non-stick baking paper. Wrap the tin in a large sheet of tinfoil to prevent water seeping in.

2   Melt the chocolate and butter in a saucepan over a low heat and stir until smooth. Remove from the heat and cool.

3   Using an electric whisk, beat the eggs, sugar and vanilla essence until light and foamy. Gradually beat in the melted chocolate, ground nuts and cinnamon, then pour into the prepared tin.

4   Set the foil-wrapped tin in a large roasting tin and pour in enough boiling water to come 2 cm/¾ inches up the sides of the tin. Bake in the preheated oven until the edge is set, but the centre is still soft when the tin is gently shaken. Remove from the oven and place on a wire rack to cool.

5   For the glaze, melt all the ingredients over a low heat until melted and smooth, then remove from the heat. Dip each pecan halfway into the glaze and set on a sheet of non-stick baking paper until set. Allow the remaining glaze to thicken slightly.

6   Remove the cake from the tin and invert. Pour the glaze over the cake smoothing the top and spreading the glaze around the sides. Arrange the glazed pecans around the edge of the torte. Allow to set and serve.

3

4

5

Lemony Coconut Cake

INGREDIENTS

Cuts into 10–12 slices

275 g/10 oz plain flour

2 tbsp cornflour

1 tbsp baking powder

1 tsp salt

150 g/5 oz white vegetable fat
  or soft margarine

275 g/10 oz caster sugar

grated zest of 2 lemons

1 tsp vanilla essence

3 large eggs

150 ml/¼ pint milk

4 tbsp Malibu or rum

450 g/1 lb jar lemon curd

lime zest, to decorate

For the frosting:

275 g/10 oz caster sugar

125 ml/4 fl oz water

1 tbsp glucose

¼ tsp salt

1 tsp vanilla essence

3 large egg whites

75 g/3 oz shredded coconut

1 Preheat the oven to 180°C/350°F/Gas Mark 4, 10 minutes before baking. Lightly oil and flour 2 x 20.5 cm/8 inch non-stick cake tins.

2 Sift the flour, cornflour, baking powder and salt into a large bowl and add the white vegetable fat or margarine, sugar, lemon zest, vanilla essence, eggs and milk. With an electric whisk on a low speed, beat until blended, adding a little extra milk if the mixture is very stiff. Increase the speed to medium and beat for about 2 minutes.

3 Divide the mixture between the tins and smooth the tops evenly. Bake in the preheated oven for 20–25 minutes, or until the cakes feel firm and are cooked. Remove from the oven and cool before removing from the tins.

4 Put all the ingredients for the frosting, except the coconut, into a heatproof bowl placed over a saucepan of simmering water. (Do not allow the base of the bowl to touch the water.)

5 Using an electric whisk, blend the frosting ingredients on a low speed. Increase the speed to high and beat for 7 minutes, until the whites are stiff and glossy. Remove the bowl from the heat and continue beating until cool. Cover with clingfilm.

6 Using a serrated knife, split the cake layers horizontally in half and sprinkle each cut surface with the Malibu or rum. Sandwich the cakes together with the lemon curd and press lightly.

7 Spread the top and sides generously with the frosting, swirling and peaking the top. Sprinkle the coconut over the top of the cake and gently press on to the sides to cover. Decorate the coconut cake with the lime zest and serve.

2

6

7

Coffee & Walnut Gateau with Brandied Prunes

INGREDIENTS

Cuts into 10–12 slices

For the prunes:
225 g/8 oz ready-to-eat pitted
   dried prunes
150 ml/¼ pint cold tea
3 tbsp brandy

For the cake:
450 g/1 lb walnut pieces
50 g/2 oz self-raising flour
½ tsp baking powder
1 tsp instant coffee powder
   (not granules)
5 large eggs, separated
¼ tsp cream of tartar
150 g/5 oz caster sugar
2 tbsp sunflower oil
8 walnut halves, to decorate

For the filling:
600 ml/1 pint double cream
4 tbsp icing sugar, sifted
2 tbsp coffee-flavoured liqueur

1 Preheat the oven to 180°C/350°F/Gas Mark 4, 10 minutes before baking. Put the prunes in a small bowl with the tea and brandy and allow to stand for 3–4 hours or overnight. Oil and line the bases of 2 x 23 cm/ 9 inch cake tins. Chop the walnut pieces in a food processor. Reserve a quarter of the nuts. Add the flour, baking powder and coffee and blend until finely ground.

2 Whisk the egg whites with the cream of tartar until soft peaks form. Sprinkle in one-third of the sugar, 2 tablespoons at a time, until stiff peaks form. In another bowl, beat the egg yolks, oil and the remaining sugar, until thick. Using a metal spoon or rubber spatula, alternately fold in the nut mixture and egg whites until just blended.

3 Divide the mixture evenly between the tins, smoothing the tops. Bake in the preheated oven for 30–35 minutes, or until the top of the cakes spring back when lightly pressed with a clean finger. Remove from the oven and cool. Remove from the tins and discard the lining paper.

4 Drain the prunes, reserving the soaking liquid. Dry on kitchen paper, then chop and reserve. Whisk the cream with the icing sugar and liqueur until soft peaks form. Spoon one-eighth of the cream into a pastry bag fitted with a star nozzle.

5 Cut the cake layers in half horizontally. Sprinkle each cut side with 1 tablespoon of the reserved prune-soaking liquid. Sandwich the cakes together with half of the cream and all of the chopped prunes.

6 Spread the remaining cream around the sides of the cake and press in the reserved chopped walnuts. Pipe rosettes around the edge of the cake. Decorate with walnut halves and serve.

1

5

6

Wild Strawberry & Rose Petal Jam Cake

INGREDIENTS

Cuts into 8 servings

275 g/10 oz plain flour
1 tsp baking powder
¼ tsp salt
150 g/5 oz unsalted
　butter, softened
200 g/7 oz caster sugar
2 large eggs, beaten
2 tbsp rosewater
125 ml/4 fl oz milk
125 g/4 oz rose petal or strawberry
　jam, slightly warmed
125 g/4 oz wild strawberries, hulled,
　or baby strawberries, chopped
frosted rose petals, to decorate

For the rose cream filling:

200 ml/7 fl oz double cream
25 ml/1 fl oz natural
　Greek yogurt
2 tbsp rosewater
1–2 tbsp icing sugar

1 Preheat the oven to 180°C/350°F/Gas Mark 4, 10 minutes before baking. Lightly oil and flour a 20.5 cm/8 inch non-stick cake tin. Sift the flour, baking powder and salt into a bowl and reserve.

2 Beat the butter and sugar until light and fluffy. Beat in the eggs, a little at a time, then stir in the rosewater. Gently fold in the flour mixture and milk with a metal spoon or rubber spatula and mix lightly together.

3 Spoon the cake mixture into the tin, spreading evenly and smoothing the top.

4 Bake in the preheated oven for 25–30 minutes, or until well risen and golden and the centre springs back when pressed with a clean finger. Remove and cool, then remove from the tin.

5 For the filling, whisk the cream, yogurt, 1 tablespoon of rosewater and 1 tablespoon of icing sugar until soft peaks form. Split the cake horizontally in half and sprinkle with the remaining rosewater.

6 Spread the warmed jam on the base of the cake. Top with half the whipped cream mixture, then sprinkle with half the strawberries. Place the remaining cake half on top. Spread with the remaining cream and swirl, if desired. Decorate with the rose petals. Dust the cake lightly with a little icing sugar and serve.

2

5

6

Celebration Fruit Cake

INGREDIENTS

Cuts into 16 slices

125 g/4 oz butter or margarine
125 g/4 oz soft dark brown sugar
380 g can crushed pineapple
150 g/5 oz raisins
150 g/5 oz sultanas
125 g/4 oz crystallised ginger,
  finely chopped
125 g/4 oz glacé cherries,
  coarsely chopped
125 g/4 oz mixed cut peel
225 g/8 oz self-raising flour
1 tsp bicarbonate of soda
2 tsp mixed spice
1 tsp ground cinnamon
½ tsp salt
2 large eggs, beaten

For the topping:

100 g/3½ oz pecan or walnut halves,
  lightly toasted
125 g/4 oz red, green and yellow
  glacé cherries
100 g/3½ oz small pitted prunes
  or dates
2 tbsp clear honey

1 Preheat the oven to 170°C/325°F/Gas Mark 3, 10 minutes before baking. Heat the butter and sugar in a saucepan until the sugar has dissolved, stirring frequently.

2 Add the pineapple and juice, dried fruits and peel. Bring to the boil, simmer 3 minutes, stirring occasionally, the remove from the heat to cool completely.

3 Lightly oil and line the base of a 20.5 x 7.5 cm/8 x 3 inch loose-bottomed cake tin with non-stick baking paper. Sift the flour, bicarbonate of soda, spices and salt into a bowl.

4 Add the boiled fruit mixture to the flour with the eggs and mix. Spoon into the tin and smooth the top. Bake in the preheated oven for 1¼ hours, or until a skewer inserted into the centre comes out clean. (If the cake is browning too quickly, cover loosely with tinfoil and reduce the oven temperature.)

5 Remove and cool completely before removing from the tin and discarding the lining paper.

6 Arrange the nuts, cherries and prunes or dates in an attractive pattern on top of the cake. Heat the honey and brush over the topping to glaze.

7 Alternatively, toss the nuts and fruits in the warm honey and spread evenly over the top of the cake. Cool completely and store in a cake tin for a day or two before serving to allow the flavours to develop.

2

4

6

Toffee Walnut Swiss Roll

INGREDIENTS

Cuts into 10–12 slices

4 large eggs, separated
½ tsp cream of tartar
125 g/4 oz icing sugar, plus
   extra to dust
½ tsp vanilla essence
125 g/4 oz self-raising flour

For the toffee walnut filling:

2 tbsp plain flour
150 ml/¼ pint milk
5 tbsp golden syrup or
   maple syrup
2 large egg yolks, beaten
100 g/3½ oz walnuts or pecans,
   toasted and chopped
300 ml/½ pint double
   cream, whipped

FOOD FACT

Using a clean tea towel to roll up the sponge in this recipe turns the steam into condensation which helps to keep the cake fairly flexible and therefore prevents it from cracking.

1. Preheat the oven to 190°C/375°F/Gas Mark 5, 10 minutes before baking. Lightly oil and line a Swiss roll tin with non-stick baking paper. Beat the egg whites and cream of tartar until softly peaking. Gradually beat in 50 g/2 oz of the icing sugar until stiff peaks form.

2. In another bowl, beat the egg yolks with the remaining icing sugar until thick. Beat in the vanilla essence. Gently fold in the flour and egg whites alternately using a metal spoon or rubber spatula. Do not over mix. Spoon the batter into the tin and spread evenly. Bake in the preheated oven for 12 minutes, or until well risen and golden and the cake springs back when pressed with a clean finger.

3. Lay a clean tea towel on a work surface and lay a piece of baking paper about 33 cm/13 inches long on the towel and dust with icing sugar. As soon as the cake is cooked turn out on to the paper. Peel off the lining paper and cut off the crisp edges of the cake. Starting at one narrow end, roll the cake with the paper and towel. Transfer to a wire rack and cool completely.

4. For the filling, put the flour, milk and syrup into a small pan and place over a gentle heat. Bring to the boil, whisking until thick and smooth. Remove from the heat and slowly beat into the beaten egg yolks.

5. Pour the mixture back into the saucepan and cook over a low heat until it thickens and coats the back of a spoon.

6. Strain the mixture into a bowl and stir in the chopped walnuts or pecans. Cool, stirring occasionally, then fold in about half of the whipped cream.

7. Unroll the cake and spread the filling over the cake. Re-roll and decorate with the remaining cream. Sprinkle with the icing sugar and serve.

1

2

3

Raspberry & Hazelnut Meringue Cake

INGREDIENTS

Cuts into 8 slices

For the meringue:

4 large egg whites

¼ tsp cream of tartar

225 g/8 oz caster sugar

75 g/3 oz hazelnuts, skinned, toasted
and finely ground

For the filling:

300 ml/½ pint double cream

1 tbsp icing sugar

1–2 tbsp raspberry-flavoured
liqueur (optional)

350 g/12 oz fresh raspberries

HELPFUL HINT

It is essential when whisking egg whites that the bowl being used is completely clean and dry, as any grease or oil will prevent the egg whites from gaining the volume needed.

1 Preheat the oven to 140°C/275°F/Gas Mark 1. Line 2 baking sheets with non-stick baking paper and draw a 20.5 cm/8 inch circle on each. Whisk the egg whites and cream of tartar until soft peaks form then gradually beat in the sugar, 2 tablespoons at a time.

2 Beat well after each addition until the whites are stiff and glossy. Using a metal spoon or rubber spatula, gently fold in the ground hazelnuts.

3 Divide the mixture evenly between the 2 circles and spread neatly. Swirl 1 of the circles to make a decorative top layer. Bake in the preheated oven for about 1½ hours, until crisp and dry. Turn off the oven and allow the meringues to cool for 1 hour. Transfer to a wire rack to cool completely. Carefully peel off the papers.

4 For the filling, whip the cream, icing sugar and liqueur, if using, together until soft peaks form. Place the flat round on a serving plate. Spread over most of the cream, reserving some for decorating and arrange the raspberries in concentric circles over the cream.

5 Place the swirly meringue on top of the cream and raspberries, pressing down gently. Pipe the remaining cream on to the meringue and decorate with a few raspberries and serve.

2

3

4

Chocolate & Almond Daquoise with Summer Berries

INGREDIENTS

Cuts into 8 servings

For the almond meringues:

6 large egg whites

¼ tsp cream of tartar

275 g/10 oz caster sugar

½ tsp almond essence

50 g/2 oz blanched or flaked almonds, lightly toasted and finely ground

For the chocolate buttercream:

75 g/3 oz butter, softened

450 g/1 lb icing sugar, sifted

50 g/2 oz cocoa powder, sifted

3–4 tbsp milk or single cream

550 g/1¼ lb mixed summer berries such as raspberries, strawberries and blackberries

To decorate:

toasted flaked almonds

icing sugar

1 Preheat the oven to 140°C/275°F/Gas Mark 1, 10 minutes before baking. Line 3 baking sheets with non-stick baking paper and draw a 20.5 cm/8 inch round on each one.

2 Whisk the egg whites and cream of tartar until soft peaks form. Gradually beat in the sugar, 2 tablespoons at a time, beating well after each addition, until the whites are stiff and glossy.

3 Beat in the almond essence, then using a metal spoon or rubber spatula gently fold in the ground almonds.

4 Divide the mixture evenly between the 3 circles of baking paper, spreading neatly into the rounds and smoothing the tops evenly.

5 Bake in the preheated oven for about 1¼ hours or until crisp, rotating the baking sheets halfway through cooking. Turn off the oven, allow to cool for about 1 hour, then remove and cool completely before discarding the lining paper

6 Beat the butter, icing sugar and cocoa powder until smooth and creamy, adding the milk or cream to form a soft consistency.

7 Reserve about a quarter of the berries to decorate. Spread 1 meringue with a third of the buttercream and top with a third of the remaining berries. Repeat with the other meringue rounds, buttercream and berries.

8 Scatter with the toasted flaked almonds, the reserved berries and sprinkle with icing sugar and serve.

2

6

7

Orange Fruit Cake

INGREDIENTS

Cuts into 10–12 slices

For the orange cake:

225 g/8 oz self-raising flour
2 tsp baking powder
225 g/8 oz caster sugar
225 g/8 oz butter, softened
4 large eggs
grated zest of 1 orange
2 tbsp orange juice
2–3 tbsp Cointreau
125 g/4 oz chopped nuts
Cape gooseberries, blueberries,
   raspberries and mint sprigs
   to decorate
icing sugar, to dust (optional)

For the filling:

450 ml/³/₄ pint double cream
50 ml/2 fl oz Greek yogurt
¹/₂ tsp vanilla essence
2–3 tbsp Cointreau
1 tbsp icing sugar
450 g/1 lb orange fruits, such as
   mango, peach, nectarine, papaya
   and yellow plums

1   Preheat the oven to 180°C/350°F/Gas Mark 4, 10 minutes before baking. Lightly oil and line the base of a 25.5 cm/10 inch ring mould tin or deep springform tin with non-stick baking paper.

2   Sift the flour and baking powder into a large bowl and stir in the sugar. Make a well in the centre and add the butter, eggs, grated zest and orange juice. Beat until blended and a smooth batter is formed. Turn into the tin and smooth the top.

3   Bake in the preheated oven for 35–45 minutes, or until golden and the sides begin to shrink from the edge of the tin. Remove, cool before removing from the tin and discard the lining paper.

4   Using a serrated knife, cut the cake horizontally about one-third from the top and remove the top layer of the cake. If not using a ring mould tin, scoop out a centre ring of sponge from the top third and the bottom two-thirds of the layer, making a hollow tunnel. Reserve for a trifle or other dessert. Sprinkle the cut sides with the Cointreau.

5   For the filling, whip the cream and yogurt with the vanilla essence, Cointreau and icing sugar until soft peaks form.

6   Chop the orange fruits and fold into the cream. Spoon some of this mixture on to the bottom cake layer, mounding it slightly. Transfer to a serving plate.

7   Cover with the top layer of sponge and spread the remaining cream mixture over the top and sides.

8   Press the chopped nuts into the sides of the cake and decorate the top with the Cape gooseberries, blueberries and raspberries. If liked, dust the top with icing sugar and serve.

6

7

8

Chocolate Mousse Cake

INGREDIENTS

Serves 8–10

For the cake:

450 g/1 lb plain dark
  chocolate, chopped
125 g/4 oz butter, softened
3 tbsp brandy
9 large eggs, separated
150 g/5 oz caster sugar

For the chocolate glaze:

225 ml/8 fl oz double cream
225 g/8 oz plain dark
  chocolate, chopped
2 tbsp brandy
1 tbsp single cream and white
  chocolate curls, to decorate

FOOD FACT

Wonderfully rich and delicious served with a fruity compote – why not try making cherry compote using either fresh, if in season, or otherwise tinned in fruit juice. Stone the cherries, or drain and then simmer on a low heat with a little apple juice until reduced.

1. Preheat the oven to 180°C/350°F/Gas Mark 4, 10 minutes before baking. Lightly oil and line the bases of 2 x 20.5 cm/8 inch springform tins with baking paper. Melt the chocolate and butter in a bowl set over a saucepan of simmering water. Stir until smooth. Remove from the heat and stir in the brandy.

2. Whisk the egg yolks and the sugar, reserving 2 tablespoons of the sugar, until thick and creamy. Slowly beat in the chocolate mixture until smooth and well blended. Whisk the egg whites until soft peaks form, then sprinkle over the remaining sugar and continue whisking until stiff but not dry.

3. Gently fold the egg whites into the chocolate mixture. Divide about two-thirds of the mixture evenly between the tins, tapping to distribute the mixture evenly. Reserve the remaining one-third of the chocolate mousse mixture for the filling. Bake in the preheated oven for about 20 minutes, or until the cakes are well risen and set. Remove and cool for at least 1 hour.

4. Loosen the edges of the cake layers with a knife. Using the fingertips, lightly press the crusty edges down. Pour the rest of the mousse over one layer, spreading until even. Carefully unclip the side, remove the other cake from the tin and gently invert on to the mousse, bottom side up to make a flat top layer. Discard lining paper and chill for 4–6 hours, or until set.

5. To make the glaze, melt the cream and chocolate with the brandy in a heavy based saucepan and stir until smooth. Cool until thickened. Unclip the side of the mousse cake and place on a wire rack. Pour over half the glaze and spread to cover. Allow to set, then decorate with chocolate curls. To serve, heat the remaining glaze and pour round each slice, and dot with cream.

1

2

4

Chocolate Box Cake

INGREDIENTS

Cuts into 16 slices

For the chocolate sponge:

175 g/6 oz self-raising flour

1 tsp baking powder

175 g/6 oz caster sugar

175 g/6 oz butter, softened

3 large eggs

25 g/1 oz cocoa powder

150 g/5 oz apricot preserve

cocoa powder, to dust

For the chocolate box:

275 g/10 oz plain dark chocolate

For the topping:

450 ml/³/₄ pint double cream

275 g/10 oz plain dark
  chocolate, melted

2 tbsp brandy

1 tsp cocoa powder to decorate

1 Preheat the oven to 180°C/350°F/Gas Mark 4, 10 minutes before baking. Lightly oil and flour a 20.5 cm/8 inch square cake tin. Sift the flour and baking powder into a large bowl and stir in the sugar.

2 Using an electric whisk, beat in the butter and eggs. Blend the cocoa powder with 1 tablespoon of water, then beat into the creamed mixture.

3 Turn into the tin and bake in the preheated oven for about 25 minutes, or until well risen and cooked. Remove and cool before removing the cake from the tin.

4 To make the chocolate box, break the chocolate into small pieces, place in a heatproof bowl over a saucepan of gently simmering water and leave until soft. Stir it occasionally until melted and smooth. Line a Swiss roll tin with non-stick baking paper then pour in the melted chocolate, tilting the tin to level. Leave until set.

5 Once the chocolate is set, turn out on to a chopping board and carefully strip off the paper. Cut into 4 strips, the same length as the cooked sponge, using a large sharp knife that has been dipped into hot water.

6 Gently heat the apricot preserve and sieve to remove lumps. Brush over the top and sides of the cake. Carefully place the chocolate strips around the cake sides and press lightly. Leave to set for at least 10 minutes.

7 For the topping, whisk the cream to soft peaks and quickly fold into the melted chocolate with the brandy. Spoon the chocolate whipped cream into a pastry bag fitted with a star nozzle and pipe a decorative design of rosettes or shells over the surface. Dust with cocoa power and serve.

5

6

7

Chocolate Creams

INGREDIENTS

Serves 4

125 g/4 oz plain dark chocolate
1 tbsp brandy
4 medium eggs, separated
200 ml/7 fl oz pint double cream
1 tbsp caster sugar
grated rind of 1 orange
2 tbsp Cointreau
25 g/1 oz white chocolate
8 physalis, to decorate

FOOD FACT

Physalis are also known as cape gooseberries. They are small, shiny, orange fruits that come in papery husks. Simply peel back the papery husks to reveal the fruit and use to decorate all sorts of desserts and fruit salads.

1 Break the chocolate into small pieces, then place in a heatproof bowl set over a saucepan of gently simmering water. Add the brandy and heat gently, stirring occasionally until the chocolate has melted and is smooth. Remove from the heat and leave to cool slightly, then beat in the egg yolks, 1 at a time, beating well after each addition. Reserve.

2 Whisk the egg whites until stiff but not dry, then stir 1 tablespoon into the chocolate mixture. Add the remainder and stir in gently. Chill in the refrigerator while preparing the cream.

3 Whip the cream until just beginning to thicken, then stir in the sugar, orange rind and Cointreau and continue to whisk together until soft peaks form. Spoon the chocolate mousse into the cream mixture and using a metal spoon, fold the 2 mixtures together to create a marbled effect. Alternatively, continue folding the 2 mixtures together until mixed thoroughly. Spoon into 4 individual glass dishes, cover each dessert with clingfilm and chill in the refrigerator for 2 hours.

4 Using a potato peeler, shave the white chocolate into curls. Uncover the desserts and scatter over the shavings. Peel the husks back from the physalis berries and pinch together for decoration. Top each dessert with 2 berries and chill in the refrigerator until ready to serve.

2

3

4

Spicy White Chocolate Mousse

INGREDIENTS

Serves 4–6

6 cardamom pods
125 ml/4 fl oz milk
3 bay leaves
200 g/7 oz white chocolate
300 ml/½ pint double cream
3 medium egg whites
1–2 tsp cocoa powder, sifted,
  for dusting

1   Tap the cardamom pods lightly so they split. Remove the seeds, then, using a pestle and mortar, crush lightly. Pour the milk into a small saucepan and add the crushed seeds and the bay leaves. Bring to the boil gently over a medium heat. Remove from the heat, cover and leave in a warm place for at least 30 minutes to infuse.

2   Break the chocolate into small pieces and place in a heatproof bowl set over a saucepan of gently simmering water. Ensure the water is not touching the base of the bowl. When the chocolate has melted remove the bowl from the heat and stir until smooth.

3   Whip the cream until it has slightly thickened and holds its shape, but does not form peaks. Reserve. Whisk the egg whites in a clean, grease-free bowl until stiff and standing in soft peaks.

4   Strain the milk through a sieve into the cooled, melted chocolate and beat until smooth. Spoon the chocolate mixture into the egg whites, then using a large metal spoon, fold gently. Add the whipped cream and fold in gently.

5   Spoon into a large serving dish or individual small cups. Chill in the refrigerator for 3–4 hours. Just before serving, dust with a little sifted cocoa powder and then serve.

TASTY TIP

Chocolate and spices go together very well as this recipe demonstrates. White chocolate has an affinity with spices such as cardamom, while dark and milk chocolate go very well with cinnamon.

2

3

4

Iced Chocolate & Raspberry Mousse

INGREDIENTS

Serves 4

12 sponge finger biscuits
juice of 2 oranges
2 tbsp Grand Marnier
300 ml/½ pint double cream
175 g/6 oz plain dark chocolate,
  broken into small pieces
225 g/8 oz frozen raspberries
6 tbsp icing sugar, sifted
cocoa powder, for dusting

To decorate:
few fresh whole raspberries
few mint leaves
grated white chocolate

1 Break the sponge finger biscuits into small pieces and divide between 4 individual glass dishes. Blend together the orange juice and Grand Marnier, then drizzle evenly over the sponge fingers. Cover with clingfilm and chill in the refrigerator for 30 minutes.

2 Meanwhile, place the cream in a small heavy-based saucepan and heat gently, stirring occasionally until boiling. Remove the saucepan from the heat then add the pieces of dark chocolate and leave to stand, untouched for about 7 minutes. Using a whisk, whisk the chocolate and cream together, until the chocolate has melted and is well blended and completely smooth. Leave to cool slightly.

3 Place the frozen raspberries and icing sugar into a food processor or liquidizer and blend until roughly crushed.

4 Fold the crushed raspberries into the cream and chocolate mixture and mix lightly until well blended. Spoon over the chilled sponge finger biscuits. Lightly dust with a little cocoa powder and decorate with whole raspberries, mint leaves and grated white chocolate. Serve immediately.

HELPFUL HINT
Remove the raspberries from the freezer about 20 minutes before you need to purée them. This will soften them slightly but they will still be frozen.

1

2

3

Chocolate Chip Ice Cream

INGREDIENTS

Serves 4

350 g/12 oz fresh raspberries,
  or thawed if frozen

25 g/1 oz icing sugar, or to taste

2 tbsp lemon juice

600 ml/1 pint milk

1 vanilla pod, seeds removed

6 medium egg yolks

125 g/4 oz caster sugar

450 g/1 lb plain dark chocolate

150 ml/¼ pint double cream

fresh fruit of your choice, to serve

HELPFUL HINT

If you prefer, you can use a food processor to beat the ice cream as described in step 6.

1 Set the freezer to rapid freeze. Simmer the raspberries with the sugar and lemon juice for 5 minutes. Leave to cool, then purée in a food processor. Press through a fine sieve to remove the pips. Reserve the coulis.

2 Pour the milk into a heavy-based saucepan and add the vanilla pod. Bring slowly to the boil, then remove from the heat and leave to infuse for 30 minutes. Remove the pod.

3 Whisk the egg yolks and caster sugar together until pale and creamy, then gradually whisk in the infused milk. Strain the mixture into a clean saucepan, place over a gentle heat and bring slowly to the boil. Cook over a gentle heat, stirring constantly, until the mixture thickens and coats the back of a wooden spoon. Do not let the mixture boil otherwise it will curdle. Once thickened, cover with clingfilm and leave the custard to cool completely.

4 Break half the chocolate into small pieces and place in a heatproof bowl set over a saucepan of gently simmering water. Heat gently, stirring frequently, until the chocolate has melted and smooth. Remove from the heat and leave to cool.

5 Whip the cream until soft peaks form and fold into the cooled custard. Roughly chop the remaining chocolate and stir into the custard mixture together with the melted chocolate. Spoon into a suitable container and freeze for 1 hour.

6 Remove from the freezer and beat well to break up all the ice crystals. Repeat the beating and freezing process twice more, then freeze for 4 hours or until the ice cream is solid. Allow to soften in the refrigerator for 30 minutes before serving with fresh fruit and the raspberry coulis. Remember to return the freezer to its normal setting.

1

3

5

Rich Chocolate & Orange Mousse Dessert

INGREDIENTS

Serves 8

8–12 sponge finger biscuits
225 g/8 oz plain dark chocolate,
  broken into pieces
225 g/8 oz unsalted butter
2 tbsp orange flower water
40 g/1½ oz cocoa powder, sifted
125 g/4 oz icing sugar, sifted
5 medium eggs, separated
50 g/2 oz caster sugar
1 orange, thinly sliced
300 ml/½ pint double cream

HELPFUL HINT

When filling a piping bag, try to avoid air pockets, which will making piping quite difficult.

1 Oil and line a 900 g/2 lb loaf tin with clingfilm, taking care to keep the clingfilm as wrinkle free as possible. Arrange the sponge finger biscuits around the edge of the loaf tin, trimming the biscuits to fit if necessary.

2 Place the chocolate, butter and orange flower water in a heavy-based saucepan and heat gently, stirring occasionally, until the chocolate has melted and is smooth. Remove the saucepan from the heat, add the cocoa powder and 50 g/2 oz of the icing sugar. Stir until smooth, then beat in the egg yolks.

3 In a clean grease-free bowl whisk the egg whites until stiff but not dry. Sift in the remaining icing sugar and whisk until stiff and glossy. Fold the egg white mixture into the chocolate mixture and, using a metal spoon or rubber spatula, stir until well blended. Spoon the mousse mixture into the prepared loaf tin and level the surface. Cover and chill in the refrigerator until set.

4 Meanwhile, place the caster sugar with 150 ml/¼ pint of water in a heavy-based saucepan and heat until the sugar has dissolved. Bring to the boil and boil for 5 minutes. Add the orange slices and simmer for about 2–4 minutes or until the slices become opaque. Drain on absorbent kitchen paper, reserve.

5 Trim the top of the biscuits to the same level as the mousse. Invert onto a plate and remove the tin and clingfilm.

6 Whip the cream until soft peaks form and spoon into a piping bag fitted with a star-shaped nozzle. Pipe swirls on top of the mousse and decorate with the orange slices. Chill in the refrigerator before serving.

1

2

2

Chocolate Fudge Sundae

INGREDIENTS

Serves 2

For the chocolate fudge sauce:

75 g/3 oz plain dark chocolate, broken into pieces
450ml/³/₄ pint double cream
175g/6 oz golden caster sugar
25 g/1 oz plain flour
pinch of salt
15 g/¹/₂ oz unsalted butter
1 tsp vanilla essence

For the sundae:

125 g/4 oz raspberries, fresh or thawed if frozen
3 scoops vanilla ice cream
3 scoops homemade chocolate ice cream (see page 156)
2 tbsp toasted flaked almonds
a few wafers, to serve

HELPFUL HINT

Ice cream will keep for 2 months in the freezer. It should be kept at a temperature at -18°C/0.4°F. If using homemade ice cream, allow to soften in the refrigerator for at least 30 minutes before using.

1 To make the chocolate fudge sauce, place the chocolate and cream in a heavy-based saucepan and heat gently until the chocolate has melted into the cream. Stir until smooth. Mix the sugar with the flour and salt, then stir in sufficient chocolate mixture to make a smooth paste.

2 Gradually blend the remaining melted chocolate mixture into the paste, then pour into a clean saucepan. Cook over a low heat, stirring frequently until smooth and thick. Remove from the heat and add the butter and vanilla essence. Stir until smooth, then cool slightly.

3 To make the sundae, crush the raspberries lightly with a fork and reserve. Spoon a little of the chocolate sauce into the bottom of 2 sundae glasses. Add a layer of crushed raspberries, then a scoop each of vanilla and chocolate ice cream.

4 Top each one with a scoop of the vanilla ice cream. Pour over the sauce, sprinkle over the almonds and serve with a wafer.

2

3

3

Chocolate Ice Cream

INGREDIENTS

Makes 1 litre/1³/₄ pints

450 ml/³/₄ pint single cream
200 g/7 oz plain dark chocolate
2 medium eggs
2 medium egg yolks
125 g/4 oz caster sugar
1 tsp vanilla essence
300 ml/¹/₂ pint double cream

To serve:
chopped nuts
coarsely grated white and plain
  dark chocolate
a few physalis

HELPFUL HINT

When beating the ice cream, expect it to melt a little. This is what should happen. Beating is necessary to break down any large ice crystals that have formed so that the finished ice cream is smooth rather than grainy or icy.

1 Set the freezer to rapid freeze, 2 hours before freezing. Place the single cream and chocolate in a heavy-based saucepan and heat gently until the chocolate has melted. Stir until smooth. Take care not to let the mixture boil. Remove from the heat.

2 Whisk the eggs, egg yolks and all but 1 tablespoon of the sugar together in a bowl until thick and pale.

3 Whisk the warmed single cream and chocolate mixture with the vanilla essence into the custard mixture. Place the bowl over a saucepan of simmering water and continue whisking until the mixture thickens and will coat the back of a spoon. To test, lift the spoon out of the mixture and draw a clean finger through the mixture coating the spoon. If it leaves a clean line, then it is ready.

4 Stand the bowl in cold water to cool. Sprinkle the surface with the reserved sugar to prevent a skin forming while it is cooling. Whip the double cream until soft peaks form, then whisk into the cooled chocolate custard.

5 Turn the ice cream mixture into a rigid container and freeze for 1 hour. Beat the ice cream thoroughly with a wooden spoon to break up all the ice crystals, then return to the freezer.

6 Continue to freeze the ice cream for a further hour, then remove and beat again. Repeat this process once or twice more, then leave the ice cream in the freezer until firm. Leave to soften in the refrigerator for at least 30 minutes before serving.

7 Remove from the refrigerator, then sprinkle over the chopped nuts and grated chocolate and serve with physalis. Turn the freezer back to its normal setting.

3

4

4

White Chocolate Trifle

INGREDIENTS

Serves 6

1 homemade or bought chocolate
   Swiss roll, sliced
4 tbsp brandy
2 tbsp Irish cream liqueur
425 g can black cherries, drained
   and pitted, with 3 tbsp of the
   juice reserved
900 ml/1½ pints double cream
125 g/4 oz white chocolate, broken
   into pieces
6 medium egg yolks
50 g/2 oz caster sugar
2 tsp cornflour
1 tsp vanilla essence
50 g/2 oz plain dark chocolate, grated
50 g/2 oz milk chocolate, grated

HELPFUL HINT

It is critical that the custard is not allowed to boil once the eggs have been added. Otherwise, the mixture turns to sweet scrambled eggs and is unusable. Cook over a very gentle heat, stirring constantly and testing the mixture often.

1 Place the Swiss roll slices in the bottom of a trifle dish and pour over the brandy, Irish cream liqueur and a little of the reserved black cherry juice to moisten the Swiss roll. Arrange the black cherries on the top.

2 Pour 600 ml/1 pint of the cream into a saucepan and add the white chocolate. Heat gently to just below simmering point. Whisk together the egg yolks, caster sugar, cornflour and vanilla essence in a small bowl.

3 Gradually whisk the egg mixture into the hot cream, then strain into a clean saucepan and return to the heat.

4 Cook the custard gently, stirring throughout until thick and coats the back of a spoon.

5 Leave the custard to cool slightly, then pour over the trifle. Leave the trifle to chill in the refrigerator for at least 3–4 hours, or preferably overnight.

6 Before serving, lightly whip the remaining cream until soft peaks form, then spoon the cream over the set custard. Using the back of a spoon, swirl the cream in a decorative pattern. Sprinkle with grated plain and milk chocolate and serve.

1

3

5

White Chocolate Terrine with Red Fruit Compote

INGREDIENTS

Serves 8

225 g/8 oz white chocolate
300 ml/½ pint double cream
225 g/8 oz full fat soft cream cheese
2 tbsp finely grated orange rind
125 g/4 oz caster sugar
350 g/12 oz mixed summer fruits,
   such as strawberries, blueberries
   and raspberries
1 tbsp Cointreau
sprigs of fresh mint, to decorate

HELPFUL HINT

Pour some boiled water into a tall jug and dip your knife into it for a few seconds. Dry the knife and use to slice the terrine, repeating the dipping when necessary.

1   Set the freezer to rapid freeze at least 2 hours before required. Lightly oil and line a 450 g/1 lb loaf tin with clingfilm, taking care to keep the clingfilm as wrinkle free as possible. Break the white chocolate into small pieces and place in a heatproof bowl set over a saucepan of gently simmering water. Leave for 20 minutes or until melted, then remove from the heat and stir until smooth. Leave to cool.

2   Whip the cream until soft peaks form. Beat the cream cheese until soft and creamy, then beat in the grated orange rind and 50 g/2 oz of the caster sugar. Mix well, then fold in the whipped cream and then the cooled melted white chocolate.

3   Spoon the mixture into the prepared loaf tin and level the surface. Place in the freezer and freeze for at least 4 hours or until frozen. Once frozen, remember to return the freezer to its normal setting.

4   Place the fruits with the remaining sugar in a heavy based saucepan and heat gently, stirring occasionally, until the sugar has dissolved and the juices from the fruits are just beginning to run. Add the Cointreau.

5   Dip the loaf tin into hot water for 30 seconds and invert onto a serving plate. Carefully remove the tin and clingfilm. Decorate with sprigs of mint and serve sliced with the prepared red fruit compote.

2

3

4

Chocolate Fruit Tiramisu

INGREDIENTS

Serves 4

2 ripe passion fruit

2 fresh nectarines or peaches

75 g/3 oz sponge finger biscuits

125 g/4 oz amaretti biscuits

5 tbsp amaretti liqueur

6 tbsp prepared black coffee

250 g/9 oz mascarpone cheese

450 ml/³/₄ pint fresh custard

200 g/7 oz plain dark chocolate, finely chopped or grated

2 tbsp cocoa powder, sifted

FOOD FACT

Mascarpone cheese is an Italian full fat cream cheese with a very thick, creamy texture and flavour. It is a classic ingredient of tiramisu. Here, it is mixed with some ready-made custard, which gives it a lighter texture.

1 Cut the passion fruit and scoop out the seeds and reserve. Plunge the nectarines or peaches into boiling water and leave for 2–3 minutes. Carefully remove the nectarines from the water, cut in half and remove the stones. Peel off the skin, chop the flesh finely and reserve.

2 Break the sponge finger biscuits and amaretti biscuits in half. Place the amaretti liqueur and prepared black coffee into a shallow dish and stir well. Place half the sponge fingers and amaretti biscuits into the amaretti and coffee mixture and soak for 30 seconds.

3 Lift out both biscuits from the liquor and arrange in the bases of 4 deep individual glass dishes.

4 Cream the mascarpone cheese until soft and creamy, then slowly beat in the fresh custard and mix well together.

5 Spoon half the mascarpone mixture over the biscuits in the dishes and sprinkle with 125 g/4 oz of the finely chopped or grated dark chocolate.

6 Arrange half the passion fruit seeds and the chopped nectarine or peaches over the chocolate and sprinkle with half the cocoa powder.

7 Place the remaining biscuits in the remaining coffee liqueur mixture and soak for 30 seconds, then arrange on top of the fruit and cocoa powder. Top with the remaining chopped or grated chocolate, nectarine or peach and the mascarpone cheese mixture, piling the mascarpone high in the dishes.

8 Chill in the refrigerator for 1¹/₂ hours, then spoon the remaining passion fruit seeds and cocoa powder over the desserts. Chill in the refrigerator for 30 minutes and serve.

Brandied Raisin Chocolate Mousse

INGREDIENTS

Serves 4

125 g/4 oz raisins
1 tsp soft brown sugar
3 tbsp brandy
200 g/7 oz plain dark chocolate
150 ml/¼ pint ready-made custard
300 ml/½ pint double cream
1 tbsp strong black coffee
1 medium egg white
50 ml/2 fl oz freshly whipped cream
chocolate curls, to decorate

1 Place the raisins in a bowl together with the sugar, then pour over the brandy. Stir well and cover with clingfilm. Leave to marinate overnight or until the raisins have absorbed most, or all, of the brandy. Stir occasionally during marinating.

2 Break the chocolate into small pieces and place in a small heatproof bowl set over a saucepan of gently simmering water. Heat gently, stirring occasionally, until the chocolate has melted and is smooth. Remove the bowl from the heat and leave to stand for about 10 minutes, or until the chocolate cools and begins to thicken. Using a metal spoon or rubber spatula, carefully fold in the prepared custard.

3 Whip the cream until soft peaks form and fold into the chocolate custard mixture together with the coffee. Gently stir in the brandy-soaked raisins with any remaining brandy left in the bowl.

4 Whisk the egg white in a clean, grease-free bowl, until stiff but not dry, then fold 1 tablespoon into the chocolate mixture and mix together lightly. Add the remaining egg white and stir lightly until well mixed. Spoon into 4 tall glasses and chill in the refrigerator for up to 2 hours.

5 Just before serving, pipe a swirl of whipped cream on the top of each mousse and decorate with the chocolate curls, then serve.

TASTY TIP

Look for Lexia raisins, which are particularly large and plump. They will soak up the alcohol really well.

2

3

4

Poached Pears with Chocolate Sauce

INGREDIENTS

Serves 4

300 ml/½ pint red wine

125 g/4 oz caster sugar

grated rind and juice of 1
    small orange

2 cm/1 inch piece fresh root ginger,
    peeled and chopped

4 firm pears, such as Williams
    or Conference

175 g/6 oz plain dark chocolate

150 ml/¼ pint double cream

25 g/1 oz golden granulated sugar

TASTY TIP

Look for pears that are ripe but
not soft. You can use unripe
pears. Conference pears have a
green skin even when ripe and an
elongated shape that makes them
look very elegant.

1 Pour the red wine with 150 ml/¼ pint of water into a heavy-based saucepan and stir in the sugar, the orange rind and juice with the ginger. Place over a gentle heat and bring slowly to the boil, stirring occasionally until the sugar has dissolved. Once the sugar has dissolved, boil steadily for 5 minutes, then remove from the heat.

2 Using a potato peeler, carefully peel the pears, leaving the stalks intact. If preferred, gently remove the cores from the base of each pear. (You can, if you prefer, leave the cores intact for a neater finish.) If necessary, cut a very thin slice off the base of each pear so they sit upright.

3 Carefully stand the pears in the hot syrup, return to the heat, cover with a lid and simmer gently for 20 minutes or until tender, turning the pears occasionally. Remove from the heat and leave to cool in the syrup, turning occasionally. Using a slotted spoon, transfer the pears to a large dish.

4 Strain the syrup, then bring back to the boil and boil rapidly until reduced and syrupy. Add the chocolate, cream and sugar to the saucepan and bring very slowly to the boil, stirring constantly until the chocolate has melted. Arrange the pears on serving plates and carefully spoon over the chocolate sauce. Serve immediately.

1

2

4

Chocolate Brûlée

INGREDIENTS

Serves 6

175 g/6 oz fresh raspberries
125 g/4 oz caster sugar
5 medium egg yolks
600 ml/1 pint double cream
1 tsp vanilla essence
175 g/6 oz white chocolate, chopped
6 tbsp demerara sugar

HELPFUL HINT

If your grill does not get hot enough, you could try using a small blowtorch to caramelise the sugar. Keep the flame moving slowly over the sugar until it is melted and bubbling. Leave to cool as above.

1 Hull and clean the raspberries. Rinse lightly, then leave to dry on absorbent kitchen paper. Once dry, divide the raspberries evenly between 6 x 150 ml/¼ pint ramekins or individual dishes.

2 Whisk the caster sugar and egg yolks in a large bowl until very thick. Pour the cream into a heavy-based saucepan, place over a medium-high heat and bring to the boil. Remove from the heat and gradually whisk into the egg mixture, then whisk in the vanilla essence.

3 Place the bowl over a saucepan of simmering water and cook for about 15–20 minutes, stirring frequently, or until thick and the custard coats the back of a wooden spoon.

4 Remove the bowl from the heat, add the chopped white chocolate and stir until melted and well blended. Pour over the raspberries in the ramekins and leave to cool. Cover with clingfilm and chill in the refrigerator for 6 hours or until firm.

5 Preheat the grill. Remove the ramekins from the refrigerator and sprinkle 1 tablespoon of the demerara sugar over each, ensuring that the custard is completely covered.

6 Cook under the preheated grill for 5–6 minutes, or until the sugar has melted and begun to caramelise. Remove from the grill, leave to cool slightly, then chill again in the refrigerator for at least 1 hour. Serve immediately.

Crème Brûlée with Sugared Raspberries

INGREDIENTS

Serves 6

600 ml/1 pint fresh
  whipping cream
4 medium egg yolks
75 g/3 oz caster sugar
½ tsp vanilla essence
25 g/1 oz demerara sugar
175 g/6 oz fresh raspberries

HELPFUL HINT

Most chefs use blow torches to brown the sugar in step 7, as this is the quickest way to caramelise the top of the dessert. Take great care if using a blow torch, especially when lighting. Otherwise use the grill, making sure that it is very hot and the dessert is thoroughly chilled before caramelising the sugar topping. This will prevent the custard underneath from melting.

1 Preheat the oven to 150°C/300°F/Gas Mark 2. Pour the cream into a bowl and place over a saucepan of gently simmering water. Heat gently but do not allow to boil.

2 Meanwhile, whisk together the egg yolks, 50 g/2 oz of the caster sugar and the vanilla essence. When the cream is warm, pour it over the egg mixture briskly whisking until it is mixed completely.

3 Pour into 6 individual ramekin dishes and place in a roasting tin.

4 Fill the tin with sufficient water to come halfway up the sides of the dishes.

5 Bake in the preheated oven for about 1 hour, or until the puddings are set. (To test if set, carefully insert a round bladed knife into the centre, if the knife comes out clean they are set.)

6 Remove the puddings from the roasting tin and allow to cool. Chill in the refrigerator, preferably overnight.

7 Sprinkle the sugar over the top of each dish and place the puddings under a preheated hot grill.

8 When the sugar has caramelised and turned deep brown, remove from the heat and cool. Chill the puddings in the refrigerator for 2–3 hours before serving.

9 Toss the raspberries in the remaining caster sugar and sprinkle over the top of each dish. Serve with a little extra cream if liked.

2

5

7

Chocolate Trifle

INGREDIENTS

Serves 4

1½ homemade or bought chocolate
   Swiss rolls
4 tbsp strawberry jam
3 tbsp medium sherry
3 tbsp brandy
350 g/12 oz fresh strawberries
2 small mangos, peeled, stoned
   and diced
200 g/7 oz plain dark chocolate
2 tbsp custard powder
2 tbsp granulated sugar
300 ml/½ pint full fat milk
250 g/9 oz mascarpone cheese
300 ml/½ pint double cream
15 g/½ oz toasted flaked almonds

1 Slice the chocolate Swiss roll thickly and spread each slice with a little strawberry jam. Place the Swiss roll slices in the base of a trifle dish or glass bowl. Sprinkle over the sherry and brandy and leave to stand for 10 minutes to let the sherry and brandy soak into the Swiss roll. Slice half the strawberries and scatter evenly over the Swiss roll with half the diced mangos.

2 Break the chocolate into small pieces and place in a small heatproof bowl set over a saucepan of gently simmering water. Heat gently, stirring occasionally until the chocolate has melted and is smooth and free from lumps.

3 Blend the custard powder, sugar and milk to a smooth paste in a bowl, then pour into a heavy-based saucepan. Place over a gentle heat and cook, stirring constantly, until the custard is smooth and thick. Add the melted chocolate and stir until smooth and blended. Remove from the heat and leave to cool. Stir in the mascarpone cheese.

4 Spoon the custard mixture over the fruit and chill in the refrigerator for 1 hour. Whip the cream until soft peaks form and pile over the top of the set custard. Sprinkle over the toasted flaked almonds and decorate with the remaining whole strawberries and diced mango.

TASTY TIP

If you prefer, use fresh custard. Heat gently, then stir in the chocolate and mascarpone cheese. Omit the custard powder, sugar and milk.

1

3

4

Chocolate Profiteroles

INGREDIENTS

Serves 4

For the pastry:

150 ml/¹/₄ pint water
50 g/2 oz butter
65 g/2¹/₂ oz plain flour, sifted
2 medium eggs, lightly beaten

For the custard:

300 ml/¹/₂ pint milk
pinch of freshly grated nutmeg
3 medium egg yolks
50 g/2 oz caster sugar
2 tbsp plain flour, sifted
2 tbsp cornflour, sifted

For the sauce:

175 g/6 oz soft brown sugar
150 ml/¹/₄ pint boiling water
1 tsp instant coffee
1 tbsp cocoa powder
1 tbsp brandy
75 g/3 oz butter
1 tbsp golden syrup

1. Preheat the oven to 220°C/425°F/Gas Mark 7, 15 minutes before cooking. Lightly oil 2 baking sheets. For the pastry, place the water and the butter in a heavy-based saucepan and bring to the boil. Remove from the heat and beat in the flour. Return to the heat and cook for 1 minute or until the mixture forms a ball in the centre of the saucepan.

2. Remove from the heat and leave to cool slightly, then gradually beat in the eggs a little at a time, beating well after each addition. Once all the eggs have been added, beat until the paste is smooth and glossy. Pipe or spoon 20 small balls onto the baking sheets, allowing plenty of room for expansion.

3. Bake in the preheated oven for 25 minutes or until well risen and golden brown. Reduce the oven temperature to 180°C/ 350°F/Gas Mark 4. Make a hole in each ball and continue to bake for a further 5 minutes. Remove from the oven and leave to cool.

4. For the custard, place the milk and nutmeg in a heavy-based saucepan and bring to the boil. In another saucepan, whisk together the egg yolks, sugar and the flours, then beat in the hot milk. Bring to the boil and simmer, whisking constantly for 2 minutes. Cover and leave to cool.

5. Spoon the custard into the profiteroles and arrange on a large serving dish. Place all the sauce ingredients in a small saucepan and bring to the boil, then simmer for 10 minutes. Remove from the heat and cool slightly before serving with the chocolate profiteroles.

1

2

5

White Chocolate Eclairs

INGREDIENTS

Serves 4–6

50 g/2 oz unsalted butter

60 g/2½ oz plain flour, sifted

2 medium eggs, lightly beaten

6 ripe passion fruit

300 ml/½ pint double cream

3 tbsp kirsch

1 tbsp icing sugar

125 g/4 oz white chocolate, broken
  into pieces

HELPFUL HINT

Passion fruit are readily available in supermarkets. They are small, round purplish fruits that should have quite wrinkled skins. Smooth passion fruit are not ripe and will have little juice or flavour.

1 Preheat the oven to 190°C/375°F/Gas Mark 5, 10 minutes before baking. Lightly oil a baking sheet. Place the butter and 150 ml/¼ pint of water in a saucepan and heat until the butter has melted, then bring to the boil.

2 Remove the saucepan from the heat and immediately add the flour all at once, beating with a wooden spoon until the mixture forms a ball in the centre of the saucepan. Leave to cool for 3 minutes.

3 Add the eggs a little at a time, beating well after each addition until the paste is smooth, shiny and of a piping consistency. Spoon the mixture into a piping bag fitted with a plain nozzle. Sprinkle the oiled baking sheet with water. Pipe the mixture onto the baking sheet in 7.5 cm/3 inch lengths, using a knife to cut each pastry length neatly.

4 Bake in the preheated oven for 18–20 minutes, or until well risen and golden. Make a slit along the side of each eclair, to let the steam escape. Return the eclairs to the oven for a further 2 minutes to dry out. Transfer to a wire rack and leave to cool.

5 Halve the passion fruit, and using a small spoon, scoop the pulp of 4 of the fruits into a bowl. Add the cream, kirsch and icing sugar and whip until the cream holds it shape. Carefully spoon or pipe into the eclairs.

6 Melt the chocolate in a small heatproof bowl set over a saucepan of simmering water and stir until smooth.

7 Leave the chocolate to cool slightly, then spread over the top of the eclairs. Scoop the seeds and pulp out of the remaining passion fruit. Sieve. Use the juice to drizzle around the eclairs when serving.

Chocolate & Rum Truffles

INGREDIENTS

Makes 44

For the chocolate truffles:

225 g/8 oz plain chocolate

25 g/1 oz butter, softened

2 medium egg yolks

2 tsp brandy or kirsch

2 tsp double cream

24 maraschino cherries, drained

2 tbsp cocoa powder, sifted

For the rum truffles:

125 g/4 oz plain dark chocolate

2 tbsp rum

125 ml/4 fl oz double cream

50 g/2 oz ground almonds

2 tbsp icing sugar, sifted

TASTY TIP

These truffles are so easy to make, they are great to give as gifts. Roll some in icing sugar, as above, and roll others in cocoa powder. Arrange in a gift box in a chequerboard pattern.

1. For the chocolate truffles, break the chocolate into pieces and place in a heatproof bowl set over a saucepan of gently simmering water. Leave for 20 minutes or until the chocolate has melted. Stir until the chocolate is smooth and remove from the heat. Leave to stand for about 6 minutes.

2. Beat the butter, the egg yolks, the brandy or kirsch and double cream together until smooth. Stir the melted chocolate into the butter and egg yolk mixture and stir until thick. Cover and leave to cool for about 30 minutes. Chill in the refrigerator for 1½ hours or until firm.

3. Divide the truffle mixture into 24 pieces and mould around the drained cherries. Roll in the cocoa powder until evenly coated. Place the truffles in petit four paper cases and chill in the refrigerator for 2 hours before serving.

4. To make the rum truffles, break the chocolate into small pieces and place in a heavy-based saucepan with the cream and rum. Heat gently until the chocolate has melted, then stir until smooth. Stir in the ground almonds and pour into a small bowl and chill in the refrigerator for at least 6 hours or until the mixture is thick.

5. Remove the truffle from the refrigerator and shape small spoonfuls, about the size of a cherry, into balls. Roll in the sifted icing sugar and place in petit four paper cases. Store the truffles in the refrigerator until ready to serve.

1

2

3

Chocolate Meringue Nest with Fruity Filling

INGREDIENTS

Serves 8

125 g/4 oz hazelnuts, toasted
125 g/4 oz golden caster sugar
75 g/3 oz plain dark chocolate, broken
  into pieces
2 medium egg whites
pinch of salt
1 tsp cornflour
½ tsp white wine vinegar
chocolate curls, to decorate

For the filling:

150 ml/¼ pint double cream
150 g/5 oz mascarpone cheese
prepared summer fruits, such as
  strawberries, raspberries and
  redcurrants

HELPFUL HINT

To make chocolate curls, melt the chocolate over hot water then pour onto a cool surface. Leave until just set but not hard, then using a large cook's knife or a cheese parer, push the blade at an angle across the surface of the chocolate to form curls.

1 Preheat the oven to 110°C/225°F/Gas Mark ¼, 5 minutes before baking and line a baking sheet with nonstick baking parchment. Place the hazelnuts and 2 tablespoons of the caster sugar in a food processor and blend to a powder. Add the chocolate and blend again until the chocolate is roughly chopped.

2 In a clean, grease-free bowl, whisk the egg whites and salt until soft peaks form. Gradually whisk in the remaining sugar a teaspoonful at a time and continue to whisk until the meringue is stiff and shiny. Fold in the cornflour and the white wine vinegar with the chocolate and hazelnut mixture.

3 Spoon the mixture into 8 mounds, about 10 cm/4 inches in diameter, on the baking parchment. Do not worry if they are not perfect shapes. Make a hollow in each mound, then place in the preheated oven. Cook for 1½ hours, then switch the oven off and leave in the oven until cool.

4 To make the filling, whip the cream until soft peaks form. In another bowl, beat the mascarpone cheese until it is softened, then mix with the cream. Spoon the mixture into the meringue nests and top with the fresh fruits. Decorate with a few chocolate curls and serve.

1

2

3

Chocolate Mallow Pie

INGREDIENTS

Serves 6

200 g/7 oz digestive biscuits
75 g/3 oz butter, melted
175 g/6 oz plain dark chocolate
20 marshmallows
1 medium egg, separated
300 ml/½ pint double cream

1 Place the biscuits in a polythene bag and finely crush with a rolling pin. Alternatively, place in a food processor and blend until fine crumbs are formed.

2 Melt the butter in a medium-sized sauce-pan, add the crushed biscuits and mix together. Press into the base of the prepared tin and leave to cool in the refrigerator.

3 Melt 125 g/4 oz of the chocolate with the marshmallows and 2 tablespoons of water in a saucepan over a gentle heat, stirring constantly. Leave to cool slightly, then stir in the egg yolk, beat well, then return to the refrigerator until cool.

4 Whisk the egg white until stiff and standing in peaks, then fold into the chocolate mixture.

5 Lightly whip the cream and fold three-quarters of the cream into the chocolate mixture. Reserve the remainder. Spoon the chocolate cream into the flan case and chill in the refrigerator until set.

6 When ready to serve, spoon the remaining cream over the chocolate pie, swirling in a decorative pattern. Grate the remaining dark chocolate and sprinkle over the cream, then serve.

TASTY TIP

Replace the digestive biscuits with an equal weight of chocolate-covered digestive biscuits to make a quick change to this recipe.

2

3

5

Lattice Treacle Tart

INGREDIENTS

Serves 4

For the pastry:
175 g/6 oz plain flour
40 g/1½ oz butter
40 g/1½ oz white vegetable fat

For the filling:
225 g/8 oz golden syrup
finely grated rind and juice
  of 1 lemon
75 g/3 oz fresh white breadcrumbs
1 small egg, beaten

1 Preheat the oven to 190°C/375°F/Gas Mark 5. Make the pastry by placing the flour, butter and white vegetable fat in a food processor. Blend in short sharp bursts until the mixture resembles fine breadcrumbs. Remove from the processor and place on a pastry board or in a large bowl.

2 Stir in enough cold water to make a dough and knead in a large bowl or on a floured surface until smooth and pliable.

3 Roll out the pastry and use to line a 20.5 cm/ 8 inch loose-bottomed fluted flan dish or tin. Reserve the pastry trimmings for decoration. Chill for 30 minutes.

4 Meanwhile, to make the filling, place the golden syrup in a saucepan and warm gently with the lemon rind and juice. Tip the breadcrumbs into the pastry case and pour the syrup mixture over the top.

5 Roll the pastry trimmings out on a lightly floured surface and cut into 6–8 thin strips. Lightly dampen the pastry edge of the tart, then place the strips across the filling in a lattice pattern. Brush the ends of the strips with water and seal to the edge of the tart. Brush a little beaten egg over the pastry and bake in the preheated oven for a 25 minutes, or until the filling is just set. Serve hot or cold.

TASTY TIP
Why not replace the breadcrumbs with the same amount of desiccated coconut?

1

4

5

Chocolate, Orange & Pine Nut Tart

INGREDIENTS

Cuts into 8–10 slices

For the sweet shortcrust pastry:
150 g/5 oz plain flour

½ tsp salt

3–4 tbsp icing sugar

125 g/4 oz unsalted butter, diced

2 medium egg yolks, beaten

½ tsp vanilla essence

For the filling:
125 g/4 oz plain dark
   chocolate, chopped

60 g/2½ oz pine nuts, lightly toasted

2 large eggs

grated zest of 1 orange

1 tbsp Cointreau

225 ml/8 fl oz whipping cream

2 tbsp orange marmalade

FOOD FACT
Cointreau is an orange-flavoured liqueur and is used in many recipes. You could substitute Grand Marnier or any other orange liqueur, if you prefer.

1 Preheat the oven to 200°C/400°F/Gas Mark 6, 15 minutes before baking. Place the flour, salt and sugar in a food processor with the butter and blend briefly. Add the egg yolks, 2 tablespoons of iced water and the vanilla essence and blend until a soft dough is formed. Remove and knead until smooth, wrap in clingfilm and chill in the refrigerator for 1 hour.

2 Lightly oil a 23 cm/9 inch loose-based flan tin. Roll the dough out on a lightly floured surface to a 28 cm/11 inch round and use to line the tin. Press into the sides of the flan tin, crimp the edges, prick the base with a fork and chill in the refrigerator for 1 hour. Bake blind in the preheated oven for 10 minutes. Remove and place on a baking sheet. Reduce the oven temperature to 190°C/375°F/Gas Mark 5.

3 To make the filling, sprinkle the chocolate and the pine nuts evenly over the base of the pastry case. Beat the eggs, orange zest, Cointreau and cream in a bowl until well blended, then pour over the chocolate and pine nuts.

4 Bake in the oven for 30 minutes, or until the pastry is golden and the custard mixture is just set. Transfer to a wire rack to cool slightly. Heat the marmalade with 1 tablespoon of water and brush over the tart. Serve warm or at room temperature.

1

2

3

Chocolate Pecan Pie

INGREDIENTS

Cuts into 8–10 slices

225 g/8 oz prepared shortcrust
 pastry (see page 184)
200 g/7 oz pecan halves
125 g/4 oz plain dark
 chocolate, chopped
25 g/1 oz butter, diced
3 medium eggs
125 g/4 oz light brown sugar
175 ml/6 fl oz golden syrup
2 tsp vanilla essence
vanilla ice cream, to serve

HELPFUL HINT

Store chocolate in a cool, dark, dry place. The best temperature to store it is 20°C/68°F – if warmer the chocolate will sweat.

HELPFUL HINT

The pastry case in this recipe is not baked blind, but the pie does not become soggy because of the long cooking time, which allows the pastry to become crisp.

1 Preheat the oven to 180°C/350°F/Gas Mark 4, 10 minutes before baking. Roll the prepared pastry out on a lightly floured surface and use to line a 25.5 cm/10 inch pie plate. Roll the trimmings out and use to make a decorative edge around the pie, then chill in the refrigerator for 1 hour.

2 Reserve about 60 perfect pecan halves, or enough to cover the top of the pie, then coarsely chop the remainder and reserve. Melt the chocolate and butter in a small saucepan over a low heat or in the microwave and reserve.

3 Beat the eggs and brush the base and sides of the pastry with a little of the beaten egg. Beat the sugar, golden syrup and vanilla essence into the beaten eggs. Add the pecans, then beat in the chocolate mixture.

4 Pour the filling into the pastry case and arrange the reserved pecan halves in concentric circles over the top. Bake in the preheated oven for 45–55 minutes, or until the filling is well risen and just set. If the pastry edge begins to brown too quickly, cover with strips of tinfoil. Remove from the oven and serve with ice cream.

1

3

4

Pear & Chocolate Custard Tart

INGREDIENTS

Cuts into 6–8 slices

For the chocolate pastry:

125 g/4 oz unsalted butter, softened

60 g/2½ oz caster sugar

2 tsp vanilla essence

175 g/6 oz plain flour, sifted

40 g/1½ oz cocoa powder

whipped cream, to serve

For the filling:

125 g/4 oz plain dark
  chocolate, chopped

225 ml/8 fl oz whipping cream

50 g/2 oz caster sugar

1 large egg

1 large egg yolk

1 tbsp crème de cacao

3 ripe pears

HELPFUL HINT

The chocolate pastry is very soft so rolling it between sheets of cling film will make it much easier to handle without having to add a lot of extra flour.

1 Preheat the oven to 190°C/375°F/Gas Mark 5, 10 minutes before baking. To make the pastry, put the butter, sugar and vanilla essence into a food processor and blend until creamy. Add the flour and cocoa powder and process until a soft dough forms. Remove the dough, wrap in clingfilm and chill in the refrigerator for at least 1 hour.

2 Roll out the dough between 2 sheets of clingfilm to a 28 cm/11 inch round. Peel off the top sheet of clingfilm and invert the pastry round into a lightly oiled 23 cm/9 inch loose-based flan tin, easing the dough into the base and sides. Prick the base with a fork, then chill in the refrigerator for 1 hour.

3 Place a sheet of nonstick baking paper and baking beans in the case and bake blind in the preheated oven for 10 minutes. Remove the paper and beans and bake for a further 5 minutes. Remove and cool.

4 To make the filling, heat the chocolate, cream and half the sugar in a medium saucepan over a low heat, stirring until melted andsmooth. Remove from the heat and cool slightly before beating in the egg, egg yolk and crème de cacao. Spread evenly over the pastry case base.

5 Peel the pears, then cut each pear in half and carefully remove the core. Cut each half crossways into thin slices and arrange over the custard, gently fanning the slices towards the centre and pressing into the chocolate custard. Bake in the oven for 10 minutes.

6 Reduce the oven temperature to 180°C/350°F/Gas Mark 4 and sprinkle the surface evenly with the remaining sugar. Bake in the oven for 20–25 minutes, or until the custard is set and the pears are tender and glazed. Remove from the oven and leave to cool slightly. Cut into slices, then serve with spoonfuls of whipped cream.

1

2

5

Hazelnut Meringues with Chocolate Sauce

INGREDIENTS

Serves 6

4 medium egg whites
225 g/8 oz caster sugar
125 g/4 oz ground hazelnuts
50 g/2 oz toasted hazelnuts, sliced
fresh berries, such as raspberries,
 strawberries and blueberries,
 to serve

For the chocolate sauce:

225 g/8 oz plain dark chocolate,
 broken into pieces
50 g/2 oz butter
300 ml/½ pint double cream
1 tbsp golden syrup

1 Preheat the oven to 150°C/300°F/Gas Mark 2, 10 minutes before baking. Line 2 baking sheets with nonstick baking parchment. Whisk the egg whites in a large grease-free bowl until stiff, then add the caster sugar, 1 teaspoonful at a time, whisking well after each addition. Continue to whisk until the mixture is stiff and dry, then using a metal spoon, fold in the ground hazelnuts.

2 Using 2 dessertspoons, spoon the mixture into 12 quenelle shapes onto the baking parchment. Sprinkle over the ground hazelnuts and bake in the preheated oven for 1½–2 hours or until dry and crisp. Switch the oven off and leave to cool in the oven.

3 To make the chocolate sauce, place the chocolate with the butter and 4 tablespoons of the cream and the golden syrup in a heavy-based saucepan and heat, stirring occasionally, until the chocolate has melted and the mixture is blended. Do not boil. Whip the remaining cream until soft peaks form.

4 Sandwich the meringues together with the whipped cream and place on serving plates. Spoon over the sauce and serve with a fresh berries.

HELPFUL HINT

It is important to add the sugar gradually when making meringues because if the sugar is not fully dissolved into the egg white it might leach out during cooking, making the meringues 'sweat'.

2

1

3

Double Chocolate Truffle Slice

INGREDIENTS

Cuts into 12–14 slices

1 quantity Chocolate Pastry
   (see page 190)
300 ml/½ pint double cream
300 g/11 oz plain dark
   chocolate, chopped
25–40 g/1–1½ oz unsalted
   butter, diced
50 ml/2 fl oz brandy or liqueur
icing sugar or cocoa powder
   for dusting
chocolate leaves, caraque or curls,
   to decorate

1   Preheat the oven to 200°C/400°F/Gas Mark 6, 15 minutes before baking. Prepare the chocolate pastry and chill in the refrigerator, according to instructions.

2   Roll the dough out to a rectangle about 38 x 15 cm/15 x 6 inches and use to line a rectangular loose-based flan tin, trim then chill in the refrigerator for 1 hour.

3   Place a sheet of nonstick baking parchment and baking beans in the pastry case, then bake blind in the preheated oven for 20 minutes. Remove the baking parchment and beans and bake for 10 minutes more. Leave to cool completely.

4   Bring the cream to the boil. Remove from the heat and add the chocolate all at once, stirring until melted and smooth. Beat in the butter, then stir in the brandy liqueur. Leave to cool slightly, then pour into the cooked pastry shell. Refrigerate until set.

5   Cut out 2.5 cm/1 inch strips of nonstick baking parchment. Place over the tart in a crisscross pattern and dust with icing sugar or cocoa.

6   Arrange chocolate leaves, caraque or curls around the edges of the tart. Refrigerate until ready to serve. Leave to soften at room temperature for 15 minutes before serving.

TASTY TIP

Liqueurs that would work very well in this recipe include Tia Maria, Kahlua, Cointreau, Grand Marnier, Amaretto and Crème de Menthe.

2

4

5

Double Chocolate Banoffee Tart

INGREDIENTS

Cuts into 8 slices

2 x 400 g cans sweetened
  condensed milk
175 g/6 oz plain dark
  chocolate, chopped
600 ml/1 pint whipping cream
1 tbsp golden syrup
25 g/1 oz butter, diced
150 g/5 oz white chocolate, grated
  or finely chopped
1 tsp vanilla essence
2–3 ripe bananas
cocoa powder, for dusting

For the ginger crumb crust:

24–26 gingernut biscuits,
  roughly crushed
100 g/3½ oz butter, melted
½ tbsp sugar, or to taste
½ tsp ground ginger

TASTY TIP

Do not assemble the tart more than 2–3 hours before serving as it will go too soft.

1   Preheat the oven to 190°C/375°F/Gas Mark 5, 10 minutes before baking. Place the condensed milk in a heavy-based saucepan and place over a gentle heat. Bring to the boil, stirring constantly. Boil gently for about 3–5 minutes or until golden. Remove from the heat and leave to cool.

2   To make the crust, place the biscuits with the melted butter, sugar and ginger in a food processor and blend together. Press into the sides and base of 23 cm/9 inch loose-based flan tin with the back of a spoon. Chill in the refrigerator for 15–20 minutes, then bake in the preheated oven for 5–6 minutes. Remove from the oven and leave to cool.

3   Melt the dark chocolate in a medium-sized saucepan with 150 ml/¼ pint of the whipping cream, the golden syrup and the butter over a low heat. Stir until smooth. Carefully pour into the crumb crust, tilting the tin to distribute the chocolate layer evenly. Chill in the refrigerator for at least 1 hour or until set.

4   Heat 150 ml/¼ pint of the remaining cream until hot, then add all the white chocolate and stir until melted and smooth. Stir in the vanilla essence and strain into a bowl. Leave to cool to room temperature.

5   Scrape the cooked condensed milk into a bowl and whisk until smooth, adding a little of the remaining cream if too thick. Spread over the chocolate layer, then slice the bananas and arrange evenly over the top.

6   Whisk the remaining cream until soft peaks form. Stir a spoonful of the cream into the white chocolate mixture, then fold in the remaining cream. Spread over the bananas, swirling to the edge. Dust with cocoa powder and chill in the refrigerator until ready to serve.

3

5

6

Chocolate Apricot Linzer Torte

INGREDIENTS

Cuts into 10–12 slices

For the chocolate almond pastry:

75 g/3 oz whole blanched almonds

125 g/4 oz caster sugar

215 g/7½ oz plain flour

2 tbsp cocoa powder

1 tsp ground cinnamon

½ tsp salt

grated zest of 1 orange

225 g/8 oz unsalted butter, diced

2–3 tbsp iced water

For the filling:

350 g/12 oz apricot jam

75 g/3 oz milk chocolate, chopped

icing sugar, for dusting

1 Preheat the oven to 375°C/190°F/Gas Mark 5, 10 minutes before baking. Lightly oil a 28 cm/11 inch flan tin. Place the almonds and half the sugar into a food processor and blend until finely ground. Add the remaining sugar, flour, cocoa powder, cinnamon, salt and orange zest and blend again. Add the diced butter and blend in short bursts to form coarse crumbs. Add the water 1 tablespoon at a time until the mixture starts to come together.

2 Turn onto a lightly floured surface and knead lightly, roll out, then using your fingertips, press half the dough onto the base and sides of the tin. Prick the base with a fork and chill in the refrigerator. Roll out the remaining dough between 2 pieces of clingfilm to a 28–30.5 cm/11–12 inch round. Slide the round onto a baking sheet and chill in the refrigerator for 30 minutes.

3 For the filling, spread the apricot jam evenly over the chilled pastry base and sprinkle with the chopped chocolate.

4 Slide the dough round onto a lightly floured surface and peel off the top layer of clingfilm. Using a straight edge, cut the round into 1 cm/½ inch strips; allow to soften until slightly flexible. Place half the strips, about 1 cm/½ inch apart, to create a lattice pattern. Press down on each side of each crossing to accentuate the effect. Press the ends of the strips to the edge, cutting off any excess. Bake in the preheated oven for 35 minutes, or until cooked. Leave to cool before dusting with icing sugar and serve cut into slices.

TASTY TIP

When making the pastry do not allow the dough to form into a ball or it will be tough.

2

3

4

Chocolate Peanut Butter Pie

INGREDIENTS

Cuts into 8 slices

22–24 chocolate wafers or peanut
  butter cookies
100 g/3½ oz butter, melted
1–2 tbsp sugar
1 tsp vanilla essence
1½ tbsp gelatine
100 g/3½ oz caster sugar
1 tbsp cornflour
½ tsp salt
225 ml/8 fl oz milk
2 large eggs, separated
2 large egg yolks
100 g/3½ oz plain dark
  chocolate, chopped
2 tbsp rum or 2 tsp vanilla essence
125 g/4 oz smooth peanut butter
300 ml/½ pint whipping cream
chocolate curls, to decorate

1 Place the wafers or cookies with the melted butter, sugar and vanilla essence in a food processor and blend together. Press into the base of 23 cm/9 inch flat tin. Chill in the refrigerator for 15–20 minutes.

2 Place 3 tablespoons of cold water in a bowl and sprinkle over the powdered gelatine, leave until softened.

3 Blend half the sugar with the cornflour and salt in a heavy-based saucepan and gradually whisk in the milk. Bring to the boil, then reduce the heat and boil gently for 1–2 minutes, or until thickened and smooth, stirring constantly.

4 Beat all the egg yolks together then whisk in half the hot milk mixture and whisk until blended. Whisk in the remaining milk mixture, return to a clean saucepan and cook gently until the mixture comes to the boil and thickens. Boil, stirring vigorously, for 1 minute, then pour a quarter of the custard into a bowl. Add the chopped chocolate and rum or vanilla essence and stir until the chocolate has melted and the mixture is smooth. Pour into the chocolate crust and chill in the refrigerator until set.

5 Whisk the softened gelatine into the remaining custard and whisk until thoroughly dissolved. Whisk in the peanut butter until melted and smooth. Whisk the egg whites until stiff, then whisk in the remaining sugar, 1 tablespoon at a time.

6 Whip the cream until soft peaks form. Fold 125 ml/4 fl oz of the cream into the custard, then fold in the egg whites. Spread the peanut butter cream mixture over the chocolate layer. Spread or pipe over the surface with the remaining cream, forming decorative swirls. Decorate with chocolate curls and chill in the refrigerator until ready to serve.

1

3

4

Mini Pistachio & Chocolate Strudels

INGREDIENTS

Makes 24

5 large sheets filo pastry
50 g/2 oz butter, melted
1–2 tbsp caster sugar for sprinkling
50 g/2 oz white chocolate, melted,
   to decorate

For the filling:

125 g/4 oz unsalted pistachios,
   finely chopped
3 tbsp caster sugar
50 g/2 oz plain dark chocolate,
   finely chopped
1–2 tsp rosewater
1 tbsp icing sugar for dusting

1 Preheat the oven to 170°C/325°F/Gas Mark 3, 10 minutes before baking. Lightly oil 2 large baking sheets. For the filling, mix the finely chopped pistachio nuts, the sugar and dark chocolate in a bowl. Sprinkle with the rosewater and stir lightly together and reserve.

2 Cut each filo pastry sheet into 4 to make 23 x 18 cm/ 9 x 7 inch rectangles. Place 1 rectangle on the work surface and brush with a little melted butter. Place another rectangle on top and brush with a little more butter. Sprinkle with a little caster sugar and spread about 1 dessertspoon of the filling along one short end. Fold the short end over the filling, then fold in the long edges and roll up. Place on the baking sheet seam-side down. Continue with the remaining pastry sheets and filling until both are used.

3 Brush each strudel with the remaining melted butter and sprinkle with a little caster sugar. Bake in the preheated oven for 20 minutes, or until golden brown and the pastry is crisp.

4 Remove from the oven and leave on the baking sheet for 2 minutes, then transfer to a wire rack. Dust with icing sugar. Place the melted white chocolate in a small piping bag fitted with a plain writing pipe and pipe squiggles over the strudel. Leave to set before serving.

TASTY TIP

Keep the unused filo pastry covered with a clean damp tea towel to prevent it from drying out.

1

2

3

'Mars' Bar Mousse in Filo Cups

INGREDIENTS

Serves 6

6 large sheets filo pastry, thawed
   if frozen

40 g/1½ oz unsalted butter, melted

1 tbsp caster sugar

3 x 60 g/2½ oz 'Mars' bars,
   coarsely chopped

1½ tbsp milk

300 ml/½ pint double cream

1 large egg white

1 tsp cocoa powder

1 tbsp plain dark grated chocolate

chocolate sauce (see page 166), to
   serve (optional)

For the topping:

300 ml/½ pint whipping cream

125 g/4 oz white chocolate, grated

1 tsp vanilla essence

TASTY TIP

When working with filo pastry,
keep the dough that you are
not using wrapped so it does not
dry out.

1   Preheat the oven to 180°C/ 350°F/Gas Mark 4, 10 minutes before baking. Lightly oil 6 x 150 ml/¼ pint ramekins. Cut the filo pastry into 15 cm/6 inch squares, place 1 square on the work surface, then brush with a little of the melted butter, sprinkle with a little caster sugar. Butter a second square and lay it over the first at an angle, sprinkle with a little more caster sugar and repeat with 2 more pastry squares.

2   Press the assembled filo pastry into the oiled ramekin, pressing into the base to make a flat bottom and keeping the edges pointing up. Continue making the cups in this way, then place on a baking sheet and bake in the preheated oven for 10–15 minutes or until crisp and golden. Remove and leave to cool before removing the filo cups from the ramekins. Leave until cold.

3   Melt the 'Mars' bars and milk in a small saucepan, stirring constantly until melted and smooth. Leave to cool for 10 minutes, stirring occasionally.

4   Whisk the cream until thick and stir a spoonful into the melted 'Mars' bar mixture, then fold in the remaining cream. Whisk the egg white until stiff and fold into the 'Mars' bar mixture together with the cocoa powder. Chill the mousse in the refrigerator for 2–3 hours.

5   For the topping, boil 125 ml/ 4 fl oz of the whipping cream, add the grated white chocolate and vanilla essence and stir until smooth, then strain into a bowl and leave to cool. Whisk the remaining cream until thick, then fold into the white chocolate cream mixture.

6   Spoon the mousse into the filo cups, cover with the cream mixture and sprinkle with grated chocolate. Chill in the refrigerator before serving with chocolate sauce, if liked.

1

2

4

Raspberry Chocolate Ganache & Berry Tartlets

INGREDIENTS

Serves 8

1 quantity Chocolate Pastry
  (see page 190)
600 ml/1 pint whipping cream
275 g/10 oz seedless raspberry jam
225 g/8 oz plain dark
  chocolate, chopped
700 g/1½ lb raspberries or other
  summer berries
50 ml/2 fl oz framboise liqueur
1 tbsp caster sugar
crème fraîche, to serve

1 Preheat the oven to 200°C/400°F/Gas Mark 6, 15 minutes before cooking. Make the chocolate pastry and use to line 8 x 7.5 cm/3 inch tartlet tins. Bake blind in the preheated oven for 12 minutes.

2 Place 400 ml/14 fl oz of the cream and half of the raspberry jam in a saucepan and bring to the boil, whisking constantly to dissolve the jam. Remove from the heat and add the chocolate all at once, stirring until the chocolate has melted.

3 Pour into the pastry-lined tartlet tins, shaking gently to distribute the ganache evenly. Chill in the refrigerator for 1 hour or until set.

4 Place the berries in a large shallow bowl. Heat the remaining raspberry jam with half the framboise liqueur over a medium heat until melted and bubbling. Drizzle over the berries and toss gently to coat.

5 Divide the berries among the tartlets, piling them up if necessary. Chill in the refrigerator until ready to serve.

6 Remove the tartlets from the refrigerator for at least 30 minutes before serving. Using an electric whisk, whisk the remaining cream with the caster sugar and the remaining framboise liqueur until it is thick and softly peaking. Serve with the tartlets and crème fraîche.

TASTY TIP

Try substituting an equal quantity of white chocolate for the plain chocolate in this recipe, as raspberries go very well with it.

1

2

3

White Chocolate & Macadamia Tartlets

INGREDIENTS

Makes 10

1 quantity Sweet Shortcrust Pastry
  (see page 186)
2 medium eggs
50 g/2 oz caster sugar
250 ml/9 fl oz golden syrup
40 g/1½ oz butter, melted
50 ml/2 fl oz whipping cream
1 tsp vanilla or almond essence
225 g/8 oz unsalted macadamia nuts,
  coarsely chopped
150 g/5 oz white chocolate,
  coarsely chopped

1 Preheat the oven to 200°C/ 400°F/Gas Mark 6, 15 minutes before baking. Roll the pastry out on a lightly floured surface and use to line 10 x 7.5–9 cm/3–3½ inch tartlet tins. Line each tin with a small piece of tinfoil and fill with baking beans. Arrange on a baking sheet and bake blind in the preheated oven for 10 minutes. Remove the tinfoil and baking beans and leave to cool.

2 Beat the eggs with the sugar until light and creamy, then beat in the golden syrup, the butter, cream and vanilla or almond essence. Stir in the macadamia nuts. Sprinkle 100 g/3½ oz of the chopped white chocolate equally over the bases of the tartlet cases and divide the mixture evenly among them.

3 Reduce the oven temperature to 180°C/350°F/Gas Mark 4 and bake the tartlets for 20 minutes, or until the tops are puffy and golden and the filling is set. Remove from the oven and leave to cool on a wire rack.

4 Carefully remove the tartlets from their tins and arrange closely together on the wire rack. Melt the remaining white chocolate and, using a teaspoon or a small paper piping bag, drizzle the melted chocolate over the surface of the tartlets in a zig-zag pattern. Serve slightly warm or at room temperature.

FOOD FACT

Macadamia nuts come from Hawaii and are large, crisp, buttery flavoured nuts. They are readily available from supermarkets.

2

2

4

Chocolaty Puffs

INGREDIENTS

Makes 12 large puffs

For the choux pastry:

150 g/5 oz plain flour

2 tbsp cocoa powder

½ tsp salt

1 tbsp sugar

125 g/4 oz butter, cut into pieces

5 large eggs

For the chocolate cream filling:

225 g/8 oz plain dark
  chocolate, chopped

600 ml/1 pint double cream

1 tbsp caster sugar (optional)

2 tbsp crème de cacao (optional)

For the chocolate sauce:

225 g/8 oz plain dark chocolate

300 ml/½ pint whipping cream

50 g/2 oz butter, diced

1–2 tbsp golden syrup

1 tsp vanilla essence

1. Preheat the oven to 220°C/425°F/Gas Mark 7, 15 minutes before baking. Lightly oil a large baking sheet. To make the choux pastry, sift the flour and cocoa powder together. Place 250 ml/9 fl oz of water, the salt, sugar and butter in a saucepan and bring to the boil. Remove from the heat and add the flour mixture all at once, beating vigorously with a wooden spoon until the mixture forms a ball in the centre of the saucepan. Return to the heat and cook for 1 minute stirring, then cool slightly.

2. Using an electric mixer, beat in 4 of the eggs, 1 at a time, beating well after each addition. Beat the last egg and add a little at a time until the dough is thick and shiny and just falls from a spoon when tapped lightly on the side of the saucepan.

3. Pipe or spoon 12 large puffs onto the prepared baking sheet, leaving space between them. Cook in the preheated oven for 30–35 minutes, or until puffy and golden. Remove from the oven, slice off the top third of each bun and return to the oven for 5 minutes to dry out. Remove and leave to cool.

4. For the filling, heat the chocolate with 125 ml/4 fl oz of the double cream and 1 tablespoon of caster sugar, if using, stirring until smooth, then leave to cool. Whisk the remaining cream until soft peaks form and stir in the crème de cacao, if using. Quickly fold the cream into the chocolate, then spoon or pipe into the choux buns and place the lids on top.

5. Place all the ingredients for the sauce in a small saucepan and heat gently, stirring until smooth. Remove from the heat and leave to cool, stirring occasionally until thickened. Pour over the puffs and serve immediately.

1

3

5

Rice Pudding & Chocolate Tart

INGREDIENTS

Serves 8

1 quantity Chocolate Pastry
  (see page 190)
1 tsp cocoa powder for dusting

For the chocolate ganache:

200 ml/7 fl oz double cream
1 tbsp golden syrup
175 g/6 oz plain dark
  chocolate, chopped
1 tbsp butter
1 tsp vanilla essence

For the rice pudding:

1 litre/1³/₄ pints milk
¹/₂ tsp salt
1 vanilla pod
100 g/3¹/₂ oz long-grain white rice
1 tbsp cornflour
2 tbsp sugar

To decorate:

few fresh blueberries
sprigs of fresh mint

1 Preheat the oven to 200°C/ 400°F/Gas Mark 6, 15 minutes before baking. Roll the chocolate pastry out and use to line a 23 cm/9 inch flan tin. Place a sheet of nonstick baking parchment and baking beans in the tin and bake blind in the preheated oven for 15 minutes.

2 For the ganache, place the cream and golden syrup in a heavy-based saucepan and bring to the boil. Remove from the heat and add the chocolate all at once, stirring until smooth. Beat in the butter and vanilla essence, pour into the baked pastry case and reserve.

3 For the rice pudding, bring the milk and salt to the boil in a medium-sized saucepan. Split the vanilla pod and scrape the seeds into the milk and add the vanilla pod. Sprinkle in the rice, then bring to the boil. Reduce the heat and simmer until the rice is tender and the milk is creamy. Remove from the heat.

4 Blend the cornflour and sugar together, then stir in 2 tablespoons of water to make a paste. Stir a little of the hot rice mixture into the cornflour mixture, then stir the cornflour mixture into the rice. Bring to the boil and cook, stirring constantly until thickened. Set the base of the saucepan into a bowl of iced water and stir until cooled and thickened. Spoon the rice pudding into the tart, smoothing the surface. Leave to set. Dust with cocoa powder, decorate with a few blueberries and fresh mint to serve.

1

2

4

Chocolate Fruit Pizza

INGREDIENTS

Serves 8

1 quantity Sweet Shortcrust Pastry
  (see page 186)
2 tbsp chocolate spread
1 small peach, very thinly sliced
1 small nectarine, very thinly sliced
150 g/5 oz strawberries, halved
  or quartered
75 g/3 oz raspberries
75 g/3 oz blueberries
75 g/3 oz plain dark chocolate,
  coarsely chopped
1 tbsp butter, melted
2 tbsp sugar
75 g/3 oz white chocolate, chopped
1 tbsp hazelnuts, toasted
  and chopped
sprigs of fresh mint, to decorate

HELPFUL HINT

Alternatively, preheat the grill and grill the pizza until the fruits begin to caramelise and the white chocolate begins to melt, do not overheat as the white chocolate could split and become gritty.

1 Preheat the oven to 200°C/400°F/Gas Mark 6, 15 minutes before baking. Lightly oil a large baking sheet. Roll the prepared pastry out to a 23 cm/9 inch round and place the pastry round onto the baking sheet, and crimp the edges. Using a fork, prick the base all over and chill in the refrigerator for 30 minutes.

2 Line the pastry with tinfoil and weigh down with an ovenproof flat dinner plate or base of a large flan tin and bake blind in the preheated oven until the edges begin to colour. Remove from the oven and discard the weight and tinfoil.

3 Carefully spread the chocolate spread over the pizza base and arrange the peach and nectarine slices around the outside edge in overlapping circles. Toss the berries with the plain chocolate and arrange in the centre. Drizzle with the melted butter and sprinkle with the sugar.

4 Bake in the preheated oven for 10–12 minutes, or until the fruit begins to soften. Transfer the pizza to a wire rack.

5 Sprinkle the white chocolate and hazelnuts over the surface and return to the oven for 1 minute or until the chocolate begins to soften. If the pastry starts to darken too much, cover the edge with strips of tinfoil. Remove to a wire rack and leave to cool. Decorate with sprigs of fresh mint and serve warm.

1

3

3

Chocolate Lemon Tartlets

INGREDIENTS

Makes 10

1 quantity Sweet Shortcrust Pastry
  (see page 186)
175 ml/6 fl oz double cream
175 g/6 oz plain dark
  chocolate, chopped
2 tbsp butter, diced
1 tsp vanilla essence
350 g/12 oz lemon curd
225 ml/8 fl oz prepared custard sauce
225 ml/8 fl oz single cream
½ –1 tsp almond essence

To decorate:

grated chocolate
toasted flaked almonds

TASTY TIP

Lemon curd is very easy to make. In a medium-sized heatproof bowl, mix together 175 g/6 oz of caster sugar, the grated rind and juice of 2 large lemons and 4 large eggs. Add 125 g/4 oz cubed unsalted butter and place the bowl over a saucepan of gently simmering water. Stir often until thickened, about 20 minutes. Leave to cool and use as above.

1. Preheat the oven to 200°C/400°F/Gas Mark 6, 15 minutes before baking. Roll the prepared pastry out on a lightly floured surface and use to line 10 x 7.5 cm/3 inch tartlet tins. Place a small piece of crumpled tinfoil in each and bake blind in the preheated oven for 12 minutes. Remove from the oven and leave to cool.

2. Bring the cream to the boil, then remove from the heat and add the chocolate all at once. Stir until smooth and melted. Beat in the butter and vanilla essence and pour into the tartlets and leave to cool.

3. Beat the lemon curd until soft and spoon a thick layer over the chocolate in each tartlet, spreading gently to the edges. Do not chill in the refrigerator or the chocolate will be too firm.

4. Place the prepared custard sauce into a large bowl and gradually whisk in the cream and almond essence until the custard is smooth and runny.

5. To serve, spoon a little custard onto a plate and place a tartlet in the centre. Sprinkle with grated chocolate and almonds, then serve.

Fudgy Mocha Pie
with Espresso Custard Sauce

INGREDIENTS

Cuts into 10 slices

125 g/4 oz plain dark
   chocolate, chopped
125 g/4 oz butter, diced
1 tbsp instant espresso powder
4 large eggs
1 tbsp golden syrup
125 g/4 oz sugar
1 tsp ground cinnamon
3 tbsp milk
icing sugar, for dusting
few fresh strawberries, to serve

For the espresso custard sauce:

2–3 tbsp instant espresso
   powder, or to taste
225 ml/8 fl oz prepared custard sauce
225 ml/8 fl oz single cream
2 tbsp coffee-flavoured
   liqueur (optional)

1 Preheat the oven to 180°C/350°F/Gas Mark 4, 10 minutes before serving. Line with tinfoil or lightly oil a deep 23 cm/9 inch pie plate. Melt the chocolate and butter in a small saucepan over a low heat and stir until smooth, then reserve. Dissolve the instant espresso powder in 1–2 tablespoons of hot water and reserve.

2 Beat the eggs with the golden syrup, the sugar, the dissolved espresso powder, the cinnamon and milk until blended. Add the melted chocolate mixture and whisk until blended. Pour into the pie plate.

3 Bake the pie in the preheated oven for about 20–25 minutes, or until the edge has set but the centre is still very soft. Leave to cool, remove from plate then dust lightly with icing sugar.

4 To make the custard sauce, dissolve the instant espresso powder with 2–3 tablespoons of hot water, then whisk into the prepared custard sauce. Slowly add the single cream, whisking constantly, then stir in the coffee-flavoured liqueur, if using. Serve slices of the pie in a pool of espresso custard with strawberries.

2

1

4

Chocolate Pecan Angel Pie

INGREDIENTS

Cuts into 8–10 slices

4 large egg whites

1/4 tsp cream of tartar

225 g/8 oz caster sugar

3 tsp vanilla essence

100 g/3½ oz pecans, lightly toasted
 and chopped

75 g/3 oz dark chocolate chips

150 ml/¼ pint double cream

150 g/5 oz white chocolate, grated

To decorate:

fresh raspberries

dark chocolate curls

few sprigs of fresh mint

HELPFUL HINT

The meringue needs to be cooked gently at a low temperature and then allowed to cool in the oven so that it can become crisp and dry without cracking too much.

1 Preheat the oven to 110°C/ 225°F/Gas Mark 1/4, 5 minutes before baking. Lightly oil a 23 cm/9 inch pie plate.

2 Using an electric mixer, whisk the egg whites and cream of tartar on a low speed until foamy, then increase the speed and beat until soft peaks form. Gradually beat in the sugar, 1 tablespoon at a time, beating well after each addition, until stiff glossy peaks form and the sugar is completely dissolved. (Test by rubbing a bit of meringue between your fingers – if gritty, continue beating.) This will take about 15 minutes.

3 Beat in 2 teaspoons of the vanilla essence, then fold in the nuts and the chocolate chips.

4 Spread the meringue evenly in the pie plate, making a shallow well in the centre and slightly building up the sides.

5 Bake in the preheated oven for 1–1¼ hours or until a golden creamy colour. Lower the oven temperature if the meringue colours too quickly. Turn the oven off, but do not remove the meringue. Leave the oven door ajar (about 5 cm/2 inches) for about 1 hour. Transfer to a wire rack until cold.

6 Pour the double cream into a small saucepan and bring to the boil. Remove from the heat, add the grated white chocolate and stir until melted. Add the remaining vanilla essence and leave to cool, then whip until thick.

7 Spoon the white chocolate whipped cream into the pie shell, piling it high and swirling decoratively. Decorate with fresh raspberries and chocolate curls. Chill in the refrigerator for 2 hours before serving. When ready to serve, add sprigs of mint on the top and cut into slices.

2

4

6

Frozen Mississippi Mud Pie

INGREDIENTS

Cuts 6–8 slices

1 quantity Ginger Crumb Crust
  (see page 196)
600 ml/1 pint chocolate ice cream
600 ml/1 pint coffee-flavoured
  ice cream

For the chocolate topping:

175 g/6 oz plain dark
  chocolate, chopped
50 ml/2 fl oz single cream
1 tbsp golden syrup
1 tsp vanilla essence
50 g/2 oz coarsely grated white and
  milk chocolate

HELPFUL HINT

Use the best-quality ice cream that is available for this recipe. Look for chocolate ice cream with added ingredients such as chocolate chips, pieces of toffee or rippled chocolate. If preferred you can add some raspberries, chopped nuts or small pieces of chopped white chocolate to both the chocolate and coffee ice cream.

1 Prepare the crumb crust and use to line a 23 cm/9 inch loose-based flan tin and freeze for 30 minutes.

2 Soften the ice creams at room temperature for about 25 minutes. Spoon the chocolate ice cream into the crumb crust, spreading it evenly over the base, then spoon the coffee ice cream over the chocolate ice cream, mounding it slightly in the centre. Return to the freezer to refreeze the ice cream.

3 For the topping, heat the dark chocolate with the cream, golden syrup and vanilla essence in a saucepan. Stir until the chocolate has melted and is smooth. Pour into a bowl and chill in the refrigerator, stirring occasionally, until cold but not set.

4 Spread the cooled chocolate mixture over the top of the frozen pie. Sprinkle with the chocolate and return to the freezer for 1½ hours or until firm. Serve at room temperature.

1

2

4

White Chocolate Mousse & Strawberry Tart

INGREDIENTS

Cuts into 10 slices

1 quantity Sweet Shortcrust Pastry
  (see page 186)
60 g/2 1/2 oz strawberry jam
1/2 tbsp kirsch or framboise liqueur
450–700 g/1–1 1/2 lb ripe strawberries,
  sliced lengthways

For the white chocolate mousse:

250 g/9 oz white chocolate, chopped
350 ml/12 oz double cream
3 tbsp kirsch or framboise liqueur
1–2 large egg whites (optional)

HELPFUL HINT

This recipe contains raw egg whites, which should be eaten with caution by vulnerable groups including the elderly, the young and pregnant women. If you are worried, omit them from the recipe.

1   Preheat the oven to 200°C/400°F/Gas Mark 6, 15 minutes before baking. Roll the prepared pastry out on a lightly floured surface and use to line a 25.5 cm/10 inch flan tin.

2   Line with either tinfoil or nonstick baking parchment and baking beans then bake blind in the preheated oven for 15–20 minutes. Remove the tinfoil or baking parchment and return to the oven for a further 5 minutes.

3   To make the mousse, place the white chocolate with 2 tablespoons of water and 125 ml/4 fl oz of the cream in a saucepan and heat gently, stirring until the chocolate has melted and is smooth. Remove from the heat, stir in the kirsch or framboise liqueur and cool.

4   Whip the remaining cream until soft peaks form. Fold a spoonful of the cream into the cooled white chocolate mixture, then fold in the remaining cream. If using, whisk the egg whites until stiff and gently fold into the white chocolate cream mixture to make a softer, lighter mousse. Chill in the refrigerator for 15–20 minutes.

5   Heat the strawberry jam with the kirsch or framboise liqueur and brush or spread half the mixture onto the pastry base. Leave to cool.

6   Spread the chilled chocolate mousse over the jam and arrange the sliced strawberries in concentric circles over the mousse. If necessary, reheat the strawberry jam and glaze the strawberries lightly.

7   Chill the tart in the refrigerator for about 3–4 hours, or until the chocolate mousse has set. Cut into slices and serve.

3

4

6

Chocolate Raspberry Mille Feuille

INGREDIENTS

Serves 6

450 g/1 lb puff pastry, thawed
   if frozen
1 quantity Chocolate Raspberry
   Ganache (see page 206), chilled
700 g/1½ lbs fresh raspberries, plus
   extra for decorating
icing sugar for dusting

For the raspberry sauce:

225 g/8 oz fresh raspberries
2 tbsp seedless raspberry jam
1–2 tbsp caster sugar, or to taste
2 tbsp lemon juice or
   framboise liqueur

HELPFUL HINT

If you prefer, make 1 big mille feuille by leaving the 3 strips whole in step 2. Slice the finished mille feuille with a sharp serrated knife.

1 Preheat the oven to 200°C/400°F/Gas Mark 6, 15 minutes before baking. Lightly oil a large baking sheet and sprinkle with a little water. Roll out the pastry on a lightly floured surface to a rectangle about 43 x 28 cm/17 x 11 inches. Cut into 3 long strips. Mark each strip crossways at 6.5 cm/2½ inch intervals using a sharp knife; this will make cutting the baked pastry easier and neater. Carefully transfer to the baking sheet, keeping the edges as straight as possible.

2 Bake in the preheated oven for 20 minutes or until well risen and golden brown. Place on a wire rack and leave to cool. Carefully transfer each rectangle to a work surface and using a sharp knife, trim the long edges straight. Cut along the knife marks to make 18 rectangles.

3 Place all the ingredients for the raspberry sauce in a food processor and blend until smooth. If the purée is too thick, add a little water. Taste and adjust the sweetness if necessary. Strain into a bowl, cover and chill in the refrigerator.

4 Place 1 pastry rectangle on the work surface flat- side down, spread with a little chocolate ganache and sprinkle with a few fresh raspberries. Spread a second rectangle with a little ganache, place over the first, pressing gently, then sprinkle with a few raspberries. Place a third rectangle on top, flat-side up, and spread with a little chocolate ganache.

5 Arrange some raspberries on top and dust lightly with a little icing sugar. Repeat with the remaining pastry rectangles, chocolate ganache and fresh raspberries.

6 Chill in the refrigerator until required and serve with the raspberry sauce and any remaining fresh raspberries.

1

2

4

Chocolate Brioche Bake

INGREDIENTS

Serves 6

200 g/7 oz plain dark chocolate,
  broken into pieces
75 g/3 oz unsalted butter
225 g/8 oz brioche, sliced
1 tsp pure orange oil or 1 tbsp grated
  orange rind
1/2 tsp freshly grated nutmeg
3 medium eggs, beaten
25 g/1 oz golden caster sugar
600 ml/1 pint milk
cocoa powder and icing sugar
  for dusting

HELPFUL HINT

Croissants, fruit buns or fruit loaves are also suitable for this recipe. It is important that the dish is left to stand for 30 minutes before baking – do not be tempted to omit this step.

FOOD FACT

Brioche is a type of French bread, enriched with eggs, butter and sugar. It is available as a large round loaf, as a plait or in a long loaf and also as individual buns. Any type is suitable for this recipe.

1 Preheat the oven to 180°C/350°F/Gas Mark 4, 10 minutes before baking. Lightly oil or butter a 1.7 litre/3 pint ovenproof dish. Melt the chocolate with 25 g/1 oz of the butter in a heatproof bowl set over a saucepan of simmering water. Stir until smooth.

2 Arrange half of the sliced brioche in the ovenproof dish, overlapping the slices slightly, then pour over half of the melted chocolate. Repeat the layers, finishing with a layer of chocolate.

3 Melt the remaining butter in a saucepan. Remove from the heat and stir in the orange oil or rind, the nutmeg and the beaten eggs. Continuing to stir, add the sugar and finally the milk. Beat thoroughly and pour over the brioche. Leave to stand for 30 minutes before baking.

4 Bake on the centre shelf in the preheated oven for 45 minutes, or until the custard is set and the topping is golden brown. Leave to stand for 5 minutes, then dust with cocoa powder and icing sugar. Serve warm.

1

2

3

Mocha Pie

INGREDIENTS

Serves 4–6

1 x 23 cm/9 inch ready-made sweet
   pastry case

For the filling:

125 g/4 oz plain dark chocolate,
   broken into pieces
175g/6 oz unsalted butter
225 g/8 oz soft brown sugar
1 tsp vanilla essence
3 tbsp strong black coffee

For the topping:

600 ml/1 pint double cream
50 g/2 oz icing sugar
2 tsp vanilla essence
1 tsp instant coffee dissolved in
   1 tsp boiling water and cooled
grated plain and white chocolate,
   to decorate

1. Place the prepared pastry case on a large serving plate and reserve. Melt the chocolate in a heatproof bowl set over a saucepan of simmering water. Ensure the water is not touching the base of the bowl. Remove from the heat, stir until smooth and leave to cool.

2. Cream the butter, soft brown sugar and vanilla essence until light and fluffy, then beat in the cooled chocolate. Add the strong black coffee, pour into the pastry case and chill in the refrigerator for about 30 minutes.

3. For the topping, whisk the cream until beginning to thicken, then whisk in the sugar and vanilla essence. Continue to whisk until the cream is softly peaking. Spoon just under half of the cream into a separate bowl and fold in the dissolved coffee.

4. Spread the remaining cream over the filling in the pastry case. Spoon the coffee-flavoured whipped cream evenly over the top, then swirl it decoratively with a palate knife. Sprinkle with grated chocolate and chill in the refrigerator until ready to serve.

HELPFUL HINT

Using a ready-made pastry case makes this a quickly made store cupboard pie that looks very impressive.

2

3

4

Peach & Chocolate Bake

INGREDIENTS

Serves 6

200 g/7 oz plain dark chocolate
125 g/4 oz unsalted butter
4 medium eggs, separated
125 g/4 oz caster sugar
425 g can peach slices, drained
½ tsp ground cinnamon
1 tbsp icing sugar, sifted, to decorate
crème fraîche, to serve

1 Preheat the oven to 170°C/325°F/Gas Mark 3, 10 minutes before baking. Lightly oil a 1.7 litre/3 pint ovenproof dish.

2 Break the chocolate and butter into small pieces and place in a small heatproof bowl set over a saucepan of gently simmering water. Ensure the water is not touching the base of the bowl and leave to melt. Remove the bowl from the heat and stir until smooth.

3 Whisk the egg yolks with the sugar until very thick and creamy, then stir the melted chocolate and butter into the whisked egg yolk mixture and mix together lightly.

4 Place the egg whites in a clean grease-free bowl and whisk until stiff, then fold 2 tablespoons of the whisked egg whites into the chocolate mixture. Mix well, then add the remaining egg white and fold in very lightly.

5 Fold the peach slices and the cinnamon into the mixture, then spoon the mixture into the prepared dish. Do not level the mixture, leave a little uneven.

6 Bake in the preheated oven for 35–40 minutes, or until well risen and just firm to the touch. Sprinkle the bake with the icing sugar and serve immediately with spoonfuls of crème fraîche.

HELPFUL HINT

As this cake contains no flour, it has a very light texture. It is very important to fold the ingredients together very lightly otherwise the air will be knocked out of the mixture.

1

3

5

Crunchy Rhubarb Crumble

INGREDIENTS

Serves 6

125 g/4 oz plain flour
50 g/2 oz softened butter
50 g/2 oz rolled oats
50 g/2 oz demerara sugar
1 tbsp sesame seeds
½ tsp ground cinnamon
450 g/1 lb fresh rhubarb
50 g/2 oz caster sugar
custard or cream, to serve

TASTY TIP

To make homemade custard, pour 600 ml/1 pint of milk with a few drops of vanilla essence into a saucepan and bring to the boil. Remove from the heat and allow to cool. Meanwhile, whisk 5 egg yolks and 3 tablespoons of caster sugar together in a mixing bowl until thick and pale in colour. Add the milk, stir and strain into a heavy-based saucepan. Cook the custard on a low heat, stirring constantly until the consistency of double cream. Pour over the rhubarb crumble and serve.

1 Preheat the oven to 180°C/350°F/Gas Mark 4. Place the flour in a large bowl and cut the butter into cubes. Add to the flour and rub in with the fingertips until the mixture looks like fine breadcrumbs, or blend for a few seconds in a food processor.

2 Stir in the rolled oats, demerara sugar, sesame seeds and cinnamon. Mix well and reserve.

3 Prepare the rhubarb by removing the thick ends of the stalks and cut diagonally into 2.5 cm/1 inch chunks. Wash thoroughly and pat dry with a clean tea towel. Place the rhubarb in a 1.1 litre/2 pint pie dish.

4 Sprinkle the caster sugar over the rhubarb and top with the reserved crumble mixture. Level the top of the crumble so that all the fruit is well covered and press down firmly. If liked, sprinkle the top with a little extra caster sugar.

5 Place on a baking sheet and bake in the preheated oven for 40–50 minutes, or until the fruit is soft and the topping is golden brown. Sprinkle the pudding with some more caster sugar and serve hot with custard or cream.

2

3

4

Chocolate Pancakes

INGREDIENTS

Cuts into 8 slices

For the pancakes:
75 g/3 oz plain flour
1 tbsp cocoa powder
1 tsp caster sugar
1/2 tsp freshly grated nutmeg
2 medium eggs
175 ml/6 fl oz milk
75 g/3 oz unsalted butter, melted

For the mango sauce:
1 ripe mango, peeled and diced
50 ml/2 fl oz white wine
2 tbsp golden caster sugar
2 tbsp rum

For the filling:
225 g/8 oz plain dark chocolate
75 ml/3 fl oz double cream
3 eggs, separated
25 g/1 oz golden caster sugar

HELPFUL HINT
Be careful in step 3 when folding the mixture together not to overmix or the finished cake will be very heavy.

1 Preheat the oven to 200°C/400°F/Gas Mark 6, 15 minutes before cooking. To make the pancakes, sift the flour, cocoa powder, sugar and nutmeg into a bowl and make a well in the centre. Beat the eggs and milk together, then gradually beat into the flour mixture to form a batter. Stir in 50 g/2 oz of the melted butter and leave to stand for 1 hour.

2 Heat an 18 cm/7 inch nonstick frying pan and brush with a little melted butter. Add about 3 tablespoons of the batter and swirl to cover the base of the pan. Cook over a medium heat for 1–2 minutes, flip over and cook for a further 40 seconds. Repeat with the remaining batter. Stack the pancakes interleaving with greaseproof paper.

3 To make the sauce, place the mango, white wine and sugar in a saucepan and bring to the boil over a medium heat, then simmer for 2–3 minutes, stirring constantly. When the mixture has thickened add the rum. Chill in the refrigerator.

4 For the filling, melt the chocolate and cream in a small heavy-based saucepan over a medium heat. Stir until smooth, then leave to cool. Beat the egg yolks with the caster sugar for 3–5 minutes, or until the mixture is pale and creamy, then beat in the chocolate mixture.

5 Beat the egg whites until stiff, then add a little to the chocolate mixture. Stir in the remainder. Spoon a little of the mixture onto a pancake. Fold in half, then fold in half again, forming a triangle. Repeat with the remaining pancakes.

6 Brush the pancakes with a little melted butter and bake in the preheated oven for 15–20 minutes or until the filling is set. Serve hot or cold with the mango sauce.

1

2

5

Iced Bakewell Tart

INGREDIENTS

Cuts into 10 slices

For the rich pastry:

175 g/6 oz plain flour
pinch of salt
60 g/2½ oz butter, cut into
 small pieces
50 g/2 oz white vegetable fat,
 cut into small pieces
2 small egg yolks, beaten

For the filling:

125 g/4 oz butter, melted
125 g/4 oz caster sugar
125 g/4 oz ground almonds
2 large eggs, beaten
few drops of almond essence
2 tbsp seedless raspberry jam

For the icing:

125 g/4 oz icing sugar, sifted
6–8 tsp fresh lemon juice
25 g/1 oz toasted flaked almonds

TASTY TIP

It is not essential to use raspberry jam. If there is none in the store cupboard use any seedless jam available. Blackcurrant jam would work particularly well.

1 Preheat the oven to 200°C/400°F/Gas Mark 6. Place the flour and salt in a bowl, rub in the butter and vegetable fat until the mixture resembles breadcrumbs. Alternatively, blend quickly, in short bursts in a food processor.

2 Add the eggs with sufficient water to make a soft, pliable dough. Knead lightly on a floured board then chill in the refrigerator for about 30 minutes. Roll out the pastry and use to line a 23 cm/9 inch loose-bottomed flan tin.

3 For the filling, mix together the melted butter, sugar, almonds and beaten eggs and add a few drops of almond essence. Spread the base of the pastry case with the raspberry jam and spoon over the egg mixture.

4 Bake in the preheated oven for about 30 minutes, or until the filling is firm and golden brown. Remove from the oven and allow to cool completely.

5 When the tart is cold make the icing by mixing together the icing sugar and lemon juice, a little at a time, until the icing is smooth and of a spreadable consistency.

6 Spread the icing over the tart, leave to set for 2–3 minutes and sprinkle with the almonds. Chill in the refrigerator for about 10 minutes and serve.

2

3

6

Apricot & Almond Slice

INGREDIENTS

Cuts into 10 slices

2 tbsp demerara sugar

25 g/1 oz flaked almonds

400 g can apricot
   halves, drained

225 g/8 oz butter

225 g/8 oz caster sugar

4 medium eggs

200 g/7 oz self-raising flour

25 g/1 oz ground almonds

½ tsp almond essence

50 g/2 oz ready-to-eat dried
   apricots, chopped

3 tbsp clear honey

3 tbsp roughly chopped
   almonds, toasted

TASTY TIP

If fresh peaches are unavailable, use nectarines. Alternatively, use drained, tinned peach halves that have been packed in juice, rather than syrup. You can vary the filling according to personal preference – try ground almonds, caster sugar, crumbled trifle sponge cakes and lemon rind, moistened with medium sherry.

1 Preheat the oven to 180°C/350°F/Gas Mark 4. Oil a 20.5 cm/8 inch square tin and line with non-stick baking paper.

2 Sprinkle the sugar and the flaked almonds over the paper, then arrange the apricot halves cut side down on top.

3 Cream the butter and sugar together in a large bowl until light and fluffy.

4 Gradually beat the eggs into the butter mixture, adding a spoonful of flour after each addition of egg.

5 When all the eggs have been added, stir in the remaining flour and ground almonds and mix thoroughly.

6 Add the almond essence and the apricots and stir well.

7 Spoon the mixture into the prepared tin, taking care not to dislodge the apricot halves. Bake in the preheated oven for 1 hour, or until golden and firm to touch.

8 Remove from the oven and allow to cool slightly for 15–20 minutes. Turn out carefully, discard the lining paper and transfer to a serving dish. Pour the honey over the top of the cake, sprinkle on the toasted almonds and serve.

1

5

8

Strawberry Flan

INGREDIENTS

Serves 6

For the sweet pastry:

175 g/6 oz plain flour
50 g/2 oz butter
50 g/2 oz white vegetable fat
2 tsp caster sugar
1 medium egg yolk, beaten

For the filling:

1 medium egg, plus 1 extra
  egg yolk
50 g/2 oz caster sugar
25 g/1 oz plain flour
300 ml/½ pint milk
few drops of vanilla essence
450 g/1 lb strawberries, cleaned
  and hulled
mint leaves, to decorate

TASTY TIP

In the summer, why not try topping the flan with a variety of mixed fruits? If liked, heat 3 tablespoons of seedless raspberry jam with 2 teaspoons of lemon juice. Stir until smooth, then use to brush over the fruit. Allow to set before serving.

1. Preheat the oven to 200°C/400°F/Gas Mark 6. Place the flour, butter and vegetable fat in a food processor and blend until the mixture resembles fine breadcrumbs. Stir in the sugar, then with the machine running, add the egg yolk and enough water to make a fairly stiff dough. Knead lightly, cover and chill in the refrigerator for 30 minutes.

2. Roll out the pastry and use to line a 23 cm/9 inch loose-bottomed flan tin. Place a piece of greaseproof paper in the pastry case and cover with baking beans or rice. Bake in the preheated oven for 15–20 minutes, until just firm. Reserve until cool.

3. Make the filling by whisking the eggs and sugar together until thick and pale. Gradually stir in the flour and then the milk. Pour into a small saucepan and simmer for 3–4 minutes stirring throughout.

4. Add the vanilla essence to taste, then pour into a bowl and leave to cool. Cover with greaseproof paper to prevent a skin from forming.

5. When the filling is cold, whisk until smooth then pour on to the cooked flan case. Slice the strawberries and arrange on the top of the filling. Decorate with the mint leaves and serve.

2

3

5

Rich Double-crust Plum Pie

INGREDIENTS

Serves 6

For the pastry:
75 g/3 oz butter
75 g/3 oz white vegetable fat
225 g/8 oz plain flour
2 medium egg yolks

For the filling:
450 g/1 lb fresh plums,
  preferably Victoria
50 g/2 oz caster sugar
1 tbsp milk
a little extra caster sugar

HELPFUL HINT

As Victoria plums have only a short season, from August to September, it is best to use other varieties that have been imported. Alternatively buy English plums in season. Halve, store and freeze them then use as required.

1 Preheat the oven to 200°C/400°F/Gas Mark 6. Make the pastry by rubbing the butter and white vegetable fat into the flour until it resembles fine breadcrumbs or blend in a food processor. Add the egg yolks and enough water to make a soft dough. Knead lightly, then wrap and leave in the refrigerator for about 30 minutes.

2 Meanwhile, prepare the fruit. Rinse and dry the plums, then cut in half and remove the stones. Slice the plums into chunks and cook in a saucepan with 25 g/1 oz of the sugar and 2 tablespoons of water for 5–7 minutes, or until slightly softened. Remove from the heat and add the remaining sugar to taste and allow to cool.

3 Roll out half the chilled pastry on a lightly floured surface and use to line the base and sides of a 1.1 litre/ 2 pint pie dish. Allow the pastry to hang over the edge of the dish. Spoon in the prepared plums.

4 Roll out the remaining pastry to use as the lid and brush the edge with a little water. Wrap the pastry around the rolling pin and place over the plums.

5 Press the edges together to seal and mark a decorative edge around the rim of the pastry by pinching with the thumb and forefinger or using the back of a fork.

6 Brush the lid with milk, and make a few slits in the top. Use any trimmings to decorate the top of the pie with pastry leaves. Place on a baking sheet and bake in the preheated oven for 30 minutes, or until golden brown. Sprinkle with a little caster sugar and serve hot or cold.

2

4

5

Baked Apple Dumplings

INGREDIENTS

Serves 4

225 g/8 oz self-raising flour
¼ tsp salt
125 g/4 oz shredded suet
4 medium cooking apples
4–6 tsp luxury mincemeat
1 medium egg white, beaten
2 tsp caster sugar
custard or vanilla sauce, to serve

TASTY TIP

To make vanilla sauce, blend 1½ tablespoons of cornflour with 3 tablespoons of milk to a smooth paste. Bring just under 300 ml/½ pint of milk to just below boiling point. Stir in the cornflour paste and cook over a gentle heat, stirring throughout until thickened and smooth. Remove from the heat and add 1 tablespoon of caster sugar, a knob of butter and ½ teaspoon of vanilla essence. Stir until the sugar and butter have melted, then serve.

1 Preheat the oven to 200°C/ 400°F/Gas Mark 6. Lightly oil a baking tray. Place the flour and salt in a bowl and stir in the suet.

2 Add just enough water to the mixture to mix to a soft but not sticky dough, using the fingertips.

3 Turn the dough on to a lightly floured board and knead lightly into a ball.

4 Divide the dough into 4 pieces and roll out each piece into a thin square, large enough to encase the apples.

5 Peel and core the apples and place 1 apple in the centre of each square of pastry.

6 Fill the centre of the apple with mincemeat, brush the edges of each pastry square with water and draw the corners up to meet over each apple.

7 Press the edges of the pastry firmly together and decorate with pastry leaves and shapes made from the extra pastry trimmings.

8 Place the apples on the prepared baking tray, brush with the egg white and sprinkle with the sugar.

9 Bake in the preheated oven for 30 minutes or until golden and the pastry and apples are cooked. Serve the dumplings hot with the custard or vanilla sauce.

2

6

7

Jam Roly Poly

INGREDIENTS

Serves 6

225 g/8 oz self-raising flour

¼ tsp salt

125 g/4 oz shredded suet

about 150 ml/¼ pint water

3 tbsp strawberry jam

1 tbsp milk, to glaze

1 tsp caster sugar

ready-made jam sauce, to serve

TASTY TIP

To make jam sauce, warm 4 tablespoons of jam such as seedless raspberry jam with 150 ml/¼ pint of water or orange juice. Stir until smooth. Blend 2 teaspoons of arrowroot with 1 tablespoon of water or juice to a smooth paste. Bring the jam mixture to almost boiling point, then stir in the blended arrowroot. Cook, stirring until the mixture thickens slightly and clears, then serve.

1 Preheat the oven to 200°C/400°F/Gas Mark 6. Make the pastry by sifting the flour and salt into a large bowl.

2 Add the suet and mix lightly, then add the water a little at a time and mix to form a soft and pliable dough. (Take care not to make the dough too wet.)

3 Turn the dough out on to a lightly floured board and knead gently until smooth.

4 Roll the dough out into a 23 cm/9 inch x 28 cm/11 inch rectangle.

5 Spread the jam over the pastry leaving a border of 1 cm/½ inch all round. Fold the border over the jam and brush the edges with water.

6 Lightly roll the rectangle up from one of the short sides, seal the top edge and press the ends together. (Do not roll the pudding up too tightly.)

7 Turn the pudding upside down on to a large piece of greaseproof paper large enough to come halfway up the sides. (If using non-stick paper, then oil lightly.)

8 Tie the ends of the paper, to make a boat-shaped paper case for the pudding to sit in and to leave plenty of room for the roly poly to expand.

9 Brush the pudding lightly with milk and sprinkle with the sugar. Bake in the preheated oven for 30–40 minutes, or until well risen and golden. Serve immediately with the jam sauce.

5

6

8

Egg Custard Tart

INGREDIENTS

Serves 6

For the sweet pastry:

50 g/2 oz butter
50 g/2 oz white vegetable fat
175 g/6 oz plain flour
1 medium egg yolk, beaten
2 tsp caster sugar

For the filling:

300 ml/½ pint milk
2 medium eggs, plus
 1 medium egg yolk
25 g/1 oz caster sugar
½ tsp freshly grated nutmeg

HELPFUL HINT

Nowadays eggs are normally date stamped so it is possible to ensure that they are eaten when they are at their best. Another way to test if an egg is fresh is to place an uncooked egg in a bowl of water – if it lies at the bottom it is fresh; if it tilts it is older (use for frying or scrambling); if it floats, discard.

1 Preheat the oven to 200°C/400°F/Gas Mark 6. Oil a 20.5 cm/8 inch flan tin or dish.

2 Make the pastry by cutting the butter and vegetable fat into small cubes. Add to the flour in a large bowl and rub in, until the mixture resembles fine breadcrumbs.

3 Add the egg, sugar and enough water to form a soft and pliable dough. Turn on to a lightly floured board and knead. Wrap and chill in the refrigerator for 30 minutes.

4 Roll the pastry out on to a lightly floured surface or pastry board and use to line the oiled flan tin. Place in the refrigerator to reserve.

5 Warm the milk in a small saucepan. Briskly whisk together the eggs, egg yolk and caster sugar.

6 Pour the milk into the egg mixture and whisk until blended.

7 Strain through a sieve into the pastry case. Place the flan tin on a baking sheet.

8 Sprinkle the top of the tart with nutmeg and bake in the preheated oven for about 15 minutes.

9 Turn the oven down to 170°C/ 325°F/Gas Mark 3 and bake for a further 30 minutes, or until the custard has set. Serve hot or cold.

2

5

7

Caramelised Chocolate Tartlets

INGREDIENTS

Serves 6

350 g/12 oz ready-made shortcrust
   pastry, thawed if frozen

150 ml/¼ pint coconut milk

40 g/1½ oz demerara sugar

50 g/2 oz plain dark
   chocolate, melted

1 medium egg, beaten

few drops vanilla essence

1 small mango, peeled, stoned
   and sliced

1 small papaya, peeled, deseeded
   and chopped

1 star fruit, sliced

1 kiwi, peeled and sliced, or use fruits
   of your choice

1 Preheat the oven to 200°C/400°F/Gas Mark 6, 15 minutes before baking. Lightly oil 6 individual tartlet tins. Roll out the ready-made pastry on a lightly floured surface and use to line the oiled tins. Prick the bases and sides with a fork and line with nonstick baking parchment and baking beans. Bake blind for 10 minutes in the preheated oven, then remove from the oven and discard the baking beans and the baking parchment.

2 Reduce the oven temperature to 180°C/350°F/Gas Mark 4. Heat the coconut milk and 15 g/½ oz of the sugar in a heavy-based saucepan, stirring constantly until the sugar has dissolved. Remove the saucepan from the heat and leave to cool.

3 Stir the melted chocolate, the beaten egg and the vanilla essence into the cooled coconut milk. Stir until well mixed, then strain into the cooked pastry cases. Place on a baking sheet and bake in the oven for 25 minutes or until set. Remove and leave to cool, then chill in the refrigerator.

4 Preheat the grill, then arrange the fruits in a decorative pattern on the top of each tartlet. Sprinkle with the remaining demerara sugar and place the tartlets in the grill pan. Grill for 2 minutes or until the sugar bubbles and browns. Turn the tartlets, if necessary and take care not to burn the sugar. Remove from the grill and leave to cool before serving.

HELPFUL HINT

Before grilling, you may find it useful to cover the edges of the pastry with tinfoil to prevent it burning under the hot grill.

1

2

4

Chocolate & Fruit Crumble

INGREDIENTS

Serves 4

For the crumble:
125 g/4 oz plain flour
125 g/4 oz butter
75 g/3 oz light soft brown sugar
50 g/2 oz rolled porridge oats
50 g/2 oz hazelnuts, chopped

For the filling:
450 g/1 lb Bramley apples
1 tbsp lemon juice
50 g/2 oz sultanas
50 g/2 oz seedless raisins
50 g/2 oz light soft brown sugar
350 g/12 oz pears, peeled, cored
   and chopped
1 tsp ground cinnamon
125 g/4 oz plain dark chocolate, very
   roughly chopped
2 tsp caster sugar for sprinkling

TASTY TIP

Bramley apples may need more sugar than other apples but they are ideal for cooking and will form a purée very easily. If you prefer, use a dessert apple such as Golden Delicious or Granny Smith, but reduce the sugar accordingly.

1 Preheat the oven to 190°C/375°F/Gas Mark 5, 10 minutes before baking. Lightly oil an ovenproof dish.

2 For the crumble, sift the flour into a large bowl. Cut the butter into small dice and add to the flour. Rub the butter into the flour until the mixture resembles fine breadcrumbs.

3 Stir the sugar, porridge oats and the chopped hazelnuts into the mixture and reserve.

4 For the filling, peel the apples, core and slice thickly. Place in a large heavy-based saucepan with the lemon juice and 3 tablespoons of water. Add the sultanas, raisins and the soft brown sugar. Bring slowly to the boil, cover and simmer over a gentle heat for 8–10 minutes, stirring occasionally, or until the apples are slightly softened.

5 Remove the saucepan from the heat and leave to cool slightly before stirring in the pears, ground cinnamon and the chopped chocolate.

6 Spoon into the prepared ovenproof dish. Sprinkle the crumble evenly over the top then bake in the preheated oven for 35–40 minutes or until the top is golden. Remove from the oven, sprinkle with the caster sugar and serve immediately.

3

5

6

Index